ISLANDS OF INDONESIA

D0723383

An offering to Harry, Aurea, Avia, Easter, and Michael, my Children, for whom my hope is that they too, with increasing amazement, may be gladdened by the beauty of the earth.

VIOLET CLIFTON WEARING A NIAS CROWN.

ISLANDS
of
INDONESIA

BY
VIOLET CLIFTON
Authoress of 'Pilgrims to the Isles of Penance'

WITH AN
INTRODUCTION BY
LORD DUNSANY

SINGAPORE
OXFORD UNIVERSITY PRESS
OXFORD NEW YORK
1991

Oxford University Press

Oxford   New York   Toronto
Delhi   Bombay   Calcutta   Madras   Karachi
Petaling Jaya   Singapore   Hong Kong   Tokyo
Nairobi   Dar es Salaam   Cape Town
Melbourne   Auckland
and associated companies in
Berlin   Ibadan

Oxford is a trade mark of Oxford University Press

Originally published as Islands of Queen Wilhelmina
by Constable & Company Ltd., London, 1927

First issued as an Oxford University Press paperback 1991

ISBN 0 19 588987 8

Printed in Malaysia by Peter Chong Printers Sdn. Bhd.
Published by Oxford University Press Pte. Ltd.,
Unit 221, Ubi Avenue 4, Singapore 1440

INTRODUCTION

THERE stands in a Southern port to meet the trains from the North a man with so much gold braid in his cap that he brings a touch of brightness even into a railway station, and when the train comes in he will bow outside the first-class carriages and point the way to the steamer. Sometimes he may do a little more than that, and sometimes less, if he sleeps late through the sunny morning. But that bow and that wave of the arm towards the steamer may usually be counted upon ; and after that the horizons begin to reveal themselves, the leagues begin to slip by, new wonders come up every day from the South or the East, and old cares drop behind, and the sun goes on shining and shining, till one day the great deserts flash into view or the long wandering rivers, and by way of one of them one comes at length to the tropics, so abounding with myriad forms of all manner of life that they seem the Creator's workshop. It is a worthy world, a fascinating, enthralling and dazzling store of wonder, to which the man with so much gold braid in his hat has bowed and waved one on. He forgets no doubt the insignificance of his part in the journey whenever he reflects on the magnitude of the splendours to which he points the way. And so am I tempted to forget the insignificance of my humble work in bowing to the reader with this preface and pointing the way with it to those enchanted isles whose scents and colours Mrs. Clifton preserves for us here. Nor is it at all an easy thing to do to preserve those scents and colours by means of ink, so that they may be transmitted unfaded from one imagination to another, even though those islands are the ancient isles of spice that bygone mariners knew : the bookshelves of the world contain many failures to prove that it is difficult. I think the difficulty lies in this : that just as I once met in a railway carriage a couple that were completing a journey round the world, and had golf-clubs and croquet mallets even in that carriage with them, so too many travelling writers take with them throughout their journey hard prejudices and conventions about life that stick up out of their story all the way, as these golf-clubs stuck out of the rack. Throughout this book there is no sign of any such lumber in the mind of the authoress to prevent her sympathies growing simply and naturally wherever she is. *Nil humanum mihi alienum est* might well be taken by her for a motto, and I feel that these words will yet further heighten my resemblance to the man in the Southern harbour who waits for the trains, for a Latin quotation in a preface has a touch of gaudiness that is similar to all that gold braid in his cap.

Of the achieving of the head of Bos Anoa by Mr. Talbot Clifton I leave the book to speak for itself, and of many lesser things, but all of them interesting, and so fresh and new and coloured, compared with the things of our daily experience here, that flickers of a strange wind out of the East seem to reach us with the turn of every page.

When stricken down by one of those terrible fevers that waste the tropics, where abundant life and abundant death are day and night struggling continually,

Mrs. Clifton spends fewer words upon the horror of it than would many another traveller in recording that she got a tiresome cold at the Fritz.

And she does not go up against the people of these flowery isles with any apparent desire that they should adopt our industry, our morals or our machines, but rather seems to drift among their customs like a feather upon a favouring wind, like a bird's feather for lightness, but for resolution and endurance like a feather wrought out of iron.

DUNSANY.

Our fervent gratitude I express to the Koninklijke Paketvaart Maatschappij, the K. P. M. of happy memory ; and to Viscount Ullswater for letters that he gave us the which spoke " Open Sesame " for us.

CONTENTS

BOOK I

CONTENTS

CONTENTS

LIST OF ILLUSTRATIONS

BOOK I

THE WANDERER.

CHAPTER I

THE WANDER MOTIF

"Scorched with the fiery veil of separation."

There is the Wander-motif. It has inspired most of the life of the Explorer,[1] him to whom my life is linked, and though we have other music at home that now almost drowns the song of the wander theme, yet it still creeps in.

I, too, heard it very clearly during the last days of the closing year of 1911. It blended with the song of the thrushes. They did not know that this warm and gentle season was the winter, and they sang and mated though the bells were ringing in the New Year. It

[1] In my former book I gave the facts which empower me to name my husband the Explorer.

3

blew over the daisies that had thrust out of the earth
to look undismayed at the pale winter sun. Its notes
sounded in the falling leaves of the oak trees, which had
clung to their faded golden garments long after the
elms and beeches stood bare. " Like a king reigning
out of time," I thought, as I passed.

Such a lovely New Year's day that was ! The glow
and the after-glow of the evening were purple and
amber. Later, the moon, luminous lotus flower, shone
in the blue of the sky, and clouds, appearing as swans,
went by white and downy. The land that is part of us
immemorially lay palely silvered about us. It seemed
to cry out against the wander-motif.

Then, as soon as the New Year came we set out for
Eastern seas, and our old house fell asleep, with its
blinds, that looked like closed eyelids, drawn down over
the windows always so wide awake when we are there.

CHAPTER II

JAVA

Viens ! Le soleil te parle en paroles sublimes ;
Dans sa flamme implacable absorbe-toi sans fin ;
Et retourne à pas lents vers les cités infimes,
Le cœur trempé sept fois dans le néant divin."

LECONTE DE LISLE.

WE sailed over perfumed waters plumbago coloured, that pale cool blue of the sea when no breath stirs, and here and there, upon its scented level, bloomed sudden islands, strange gardens of the ocean, green with palms. So journeying, we reached Java—the Much Desired.

Conquerors came from East and West far back in time, and lately a new master subdued her, and possessed her. Then they, like the waves that on her shores beat the moon's measure, ebbed away, and another sweep of victors came up over the land.

Java has offered but a tired resistance ; instead, she has poisoned her masters with her fevers and enchanted them with her beauty, and from everyone she has taken a gift. When his little time was over, each warrior has left a Java subdued, but unchanged at heart and endowed with yet another grace learnt from her conqueror.

First came the Hindu in the sixth century, and from him she learned her slow dances of waving hands and

5

rustling feet. The ruins of his temples are the jewels of her girdle ; but the faith he taught her is forgotten, save by some few of her children, or lingers only in tales, toys, and long poetic dramas.

Next came the Arab, fiery from the desert. He forced her on to her knees, and bowed her on the palms of her hands down before Allah, and he gave her his learning and his writing, so that now his alphabet is her own. She kept his weapons. To-day she bows to Allah when the prayer-gong sounds, but in her heart she carries alive the old beliefs in a thousand spirits and powers that share the sceptre of her emasculated Allah.

Then fell on her the conqueror from Portugal, and he compelled her with sword and pain to honour Mary and her Child—but all that he left with her of his brief night of possession is the stain of his blood in some of her children, whilst in her lower speech (the speech she has kept for the trader and the traveller) some words of his Latin tongue remain.

The Netherlands afterwards poured in their hosts and at first ill-treated her. The French held Java a short time till the British owned her and gave her Raffles as her Master. He imbibed her laws, her "adat," her own beloved customs, and on them he framed a fair means of wedding her to peace.

After she had been comforted and made whole, she was given back to the men of the Netherlands, and perhaps to-day she is content ; or does she, in the silence of her soul, turn with longing to the rulers that are of her own blood, and desire in vain the return of their house ?

"SLOW DANCE OF WAVING HANDS AND RUSTLING FEET."

To face page 6.

CHAPTER III

SUMATRA

" Lo ! there are many ways and many traps,
    And many guides, and which of them is lord ?
    For verily Mahomet has the sword !
    And he may have the truth—*Perhaps ! Perhaps !* "

AT Batavia we boarded the comfortable ship which was
to convey us to Padang on the west coast of Sumatra,
for we meant to cross the island but had not yet decided
on any special route. In fact, in Java we could ascertain but little about Sumatra.

We arranged to go to Toba Meer, the home of the
Bataks, of whom we had heard strange rumours.
Talbot hoped to shoot a tiger, that being the only big
game animal which he has never killed.

We sailed the brilliant seas as far as Semangka,
a romantic hamlet in the lap of the jungle. Malays
and Chinese have settled in the village, therefore we did
not see any pure-bred Sumatrans. Tigers haunt the
hills and come into the little town. The Assistant
Resident had seen a tiger since he had seen a white
woman. When I was told how long it was since he
had seen a white woman, I regretted that I looked as
unpleasing as I did in my short khaki skirt and blue
Hungarian jacket.

7

Forward across the blazing sea again, sailing under high hills that mothered trees innumerable, we travelled on to Bencoolen. As we approached, the stern of the steamer became a stage of joyous expectation. Sumatran natives gazed out from the deck, and hours before arrival put on glad garments for this home-coming. There were Hadjis amongst them, pilgrims from Mecca, two men and two women, worthy of a new Canterbury tale as poignant as could be written.

From the sleepy heart of Bencoolen, from behind the screen of the world, these four had ventured out on European ships. They had sailed as far as Yiddah, and thence had gone on camels to Mecca, had been robbed by highwaymen, scorched by the sun, till, distracted by all the strangeness of their surroundings, they finally fell in adoration at the tomb of the Prophet. They had probably spent the total savings of their years on this journey. They had been cheated of much and had given more than they could afford for the honourable garments they were putting on, clothes which symbolised that they had been on the devout pilgrimage.

Bencoolen made me sad, because, after Raffles' occupation and many efforts, it had slipped from British hands. In 1818, he, the great Englishman, went there and freed the slaves and pacified the chiefs. Where are the latter now? Nearly all those on the west coast of Sumatra have been deposed from power. The Dutch official house of residence is still called Marlborough, and a statue on a hill speaks of the days of the British. I thought of Parr, the courageous, upright, unsympathetic administrator, who preceded Raffles. He was murdered by the natives as a protest against his rule. He would not double his guard or take warning. He was overpowered as he slept and was killed, though his wife covered him with her body and fought wildly for him. She was wounded and thrust under the bed whilst her husband was murdered. When, soon after this tragedy, she sailed for England with her children, the ship was wrecked and all aboard were lost.

Afterwards came the bitter reprisal, and the land which nature often tore with earthquakes, was mutilated by the British. Its trees, which are the very life of the village people, as well as their protecting deities, were felled to the ground.

" They shall not any more shelter enemies and hide their attacks," said the avenging British. Then like balm came Raffles and healed the old wounds, and was undervalued and flouted by those in authority at home. He wrote only in the sand, for Sumatra has passed from our keeping.

Raffles loved Java more than Sumatra. " I would not give one Java for a thousand such islands." If, after death, he saw that Java also was yielded to the Dutch whom he despised, he must have sorrowed greatly.

Bencoolen was all colour, an inhabited material rainbow. The violet foaming sea girded its gardens, bright with crotons and flowering plants, chosen especially by the people for their brilliance. The great coconut palms cast their shadows across the broad roads, gay carts ran noisily behind the rapid little ponies, harnessed with coloured trappings. In such a cart, all blue and yellow and red, I saw a woman who made a picture in my mind. She was brighter than a tulip, enfolded in gauzy veils and shining silks, in her arms was an impossible little nut-brown baby, stiff with finery. The woman's face was a perfect oval. It was a ghastly white—powdered perhaps— but her lips were carmine with betel juice. The haunted deadness of her face made my pulses weaken. She looked out of the gaudy carriage with so vacant a gaze that all intelligence seemed to have been frozen as though in the space of a stab. Her eyes were more dazed than those of a virgin of Botticelli. Had she, I wondered, just heard "talak" spoken for the third time. Terrible word that the lord of her home might three times at equal intervals call out. "Talak, I put you forth," with pauses for mercy given in between each repetition, but which three times repeated, would be her sentence of divorce.

She passed along the white road, but the memory of her stayed with me.

From a previous African photograph.

TALBOT CLIFTON.

To face page 10.

CHAPTER IV

PADANG

"Sois pieux devant le jour qui se lève. . . . Sois pieux
envers chaque jour. Aime le, respecte le, ne le flétris pas ;
surtout ne l'empêche pas de fleurir."

ROMAIN ROLLAND.

AFTER some days we reached Padang, and, from the
port, took the train to the city that lay among the hills.
Padang seemed new and somehow still untamed, though
later, when we touched there after having visited far-
off islands, it was to us the very climax of civilization.

Most of the natives wore a sarong and a white jacket,
like those of the men of Java. The people here were
not very distinctive, though of a sturdier build than the
Javanese.

On board I had learnt something of the easy bastard
Malay spoken by travellers and understood by most
of the natives in Java and in the towns of Sumatra : it
resembles the true Malay, but has an admixture of
French, Dutch, Portuguese and Spanish words.

Here Abraham, a native serving boy, came into our
lives, and I was just able to speak to him and to understand that he could not leave the town to follow us till
we had paid him a month's wages in advance to pacify
his creditors. Most of his wages had doubtless been

spent on the charming white jacket and the painted sarongs that he wore. His head was large and round, his face merry and clever. He was very important and over-independent, and had narrowly escaped long imprisonment for stabbing a boy in the Dutch Club, where he had served as billiard-marker.

Now there were five of us travelling—himself and myself, Abraham and two four-footed fidelities that, to unseeing people, appear to be merely members of that species of dumb animal called canine—simply that, and nothing more. One was my black and golden blood-hound, with the brow of a philosopher and points seemingly of gore where eyes would be in any lesser dog, long-eared, cheery tailed, and solemn-faced, with a bay like the notes of a horn. He struck terror into the hearts of the people. They did not know him for a dog, but thought him some wild beast of Europe come to devour them. Our other friend, Caddy, a spaniel, seemed also strange and terrible to them. He was a heavy-weight beside the nervy pariahs of the country, and was clothed as for arctic climes in thick brown pelt, which Nature pulled out in handfuls as we neared the tropics.

We left Padang, and travelled to Fort de Kock, some seventy miles by rail, and almost the terminus of the railway. Whichever road we chose, we must perforce pass through this city.

At evening we reached Fort de Kock. From the rounded bosom of the landscape there rose over the fields and amid the trees the beautiful roofs of the native houses, shaped, I thought, like twin moons embraced by one another, the lesser crescent lying in the curve of the greater. Afterwards we learned the meaning of these symbolic house tops, which are formed into horns to do honour to the buffalo. The inhabitants of this western part of Sumatra are called the " Minang Kerbau," the People of the Victorious Buffalo.

Long ago, so legend says, the people of Java and these men of the Sumatran hills, were for ever at war with one another, till they tired of fighting and agreed each to choose a champion to fight in their stead, that the flower of their people might not be destroyed in the unending battle. The sons of Java chose a tiger, and the men of Sumatra trusted their cause to a buffalo. The two peoples agreed that the men of the defeated nation should " go dressed as women forever." The beasts were made angry, put in the lists against each other; the buffalo won. The Javanese wear the sarong fastened about them like a skirt, but the children of Minang Kerbau wear trousers with an air of victory to this day.

This is the romance of the roof, and of the men's attire.

CHAPTER V

IN THE HILLS

" If, when he reached his journey's end,

. . . . . .

He had not gained an honest friend,
And twenty curious scraps of knowledge—
If he departed as he came . .

. . . . . .

Good sooth, the traveller was to blame."

PRAED.

WITH the help of the Governor, to whom we brought
a letter of introduction from the Governor-General in
Java, we chose our route for crossing Sumatra. We
determined to go as far as Pajakombo by rail, that being
the last station on the western railway line, and thence
by the Kampar Kanan to the Siak river, which has its
exit on the east coast. We wished to reach the east
coast that we might eventually go to the lake of Toba,
the home of the Batak people of whom we had heard
strange things—things that invited us to know them
as well as we might in a bird-of-passage manner.

We hoped to come across tiger on this river route,
but information is very difficult to obtain when travelling in the Dutch possessions. The lack of interest
evinced in the interior by the officials is most strange.
The Dutch, I have read, were in Java some hundred

14

years or so before knowing of the existence of the magnificent Hindu ruins of Boro Budur. This I can well believe. In contrast to this fact there are in Holland scientific societies for acquiring knowledge of the islands, and these have a large amount of valuable data. Officials studying for colonial positions are magnificently grounded in the knowledge of the religions they will encounter, and of national customs. As far as we saw, they seldom add very much observation to these book-learnt facts.

Baron von Hoëffel, aide-de-camp to the Governor, was making enquiries for us as to ponies and equipment, and whilst waiting for these details to be settled we determined to pass our time by going to Lake Manindjau in the hills. We therefore hired two extremely uncomfortable spring carts, and seizing what room we could after bloodhound Boffles, the inconvenient, was accommodated, we started off at dawn, and travelled for some hours to the summit of the hills.

The green of the young rice pierced the earth. Heavy surrounding cliffs rose abruptly from the fields, reaching in red ledges along to the hills. Suddenly, in the plain, a mass of unexpected rock towered like Babel hung about with mists.

Peasants breathed inharmonious, fascinating pastorals on river reeds, orchids were weeds upon our way, whilst flowers like Japanese lamps lit the hedges. The small cinnamons, aflame with their young red leaves and their spiced branches, were then at the most beautiful time of their growth. Little trees of sorrow we thought them, for in the past the greed of trade caused the Dutch to monopolise the spices of these eastern islands and to punish with death those natives who sold any for their own benefit. To raise the price of spices, they also destroyed a vast quantity of plants.

The men we met upon the road walked burdened in fairy tale way, nearly everyone carrying a bird cage in his hand. From Fort de Kock to Kotabaru, where days and days later we arrived, we saw this same fantastic sight, men walking with rhythm in their gait, and with a bird cage—perhaps a gift to a friend or as sheltering a beloved companion not to be parted with. The small round cages were covered with a bright cloth or a piece of crimson velvet. Tassels of gold thread hung from them, and within were rice birds or grey doves.

In some of the villages we saw these cages high up on poles, from whence melodious Stylites sang to the people of the little towns.

We walked most of the way to spare the ponies. They belonged to a Sumatran driver, who very much resented our ever wishing to drive.

At last we reached the Rest House where the Dutch comptroller, a Eurasian, and his wife, were living whilst their own house was being rebuilt. The young woman was refreshing to see, her beauty a consolation for the dust and heat of the way ; her face like that of a Grecian statue, framed with golden hair.

They were very kind to us.

From the Rest House we could not see the lake,

Photograph by Violet Clifton.

"THE SUMATRAN HOUSE OF MY PICTURE."

To face page 16.

though beauty lay all about us in the valley beneath and in the village near.   Among the flowers stood the Sumatran house of my picture.   It was decorated with red lacquer and mother-of-pearl; the roof was curved into noble horns.

CHAPTER VI

LAKE MANINDJAU

" When the painted birds laugh in the shade,
    When our table with cherries and nuts is spread,
    Come live, and be merry and join with me,
    To sing the sweet chorus of Ha, Ha, He ! "

                                       BLAKE.

AT dawn we were driving to the top of the hill over the lake. The Dutch had, alas ! sealed the summit with ugliness in the form of a summer house with a grey corrugated iron roof.

I felt myself crimsoning as we neared it, for this enormity was part of the western civilisation to which I belong. Whatever that civilisation may be (and, travelling, I have often wondered what, indeed, it is), it cannot be anything greater than beauty. I think many crimes, much greed, time misspent, and the dullest states of unhappiness are all the progeny of civilisation. So, also, are the heart of mercy and the hand of the Samaritan.

Still I cannot forgive the ugly roof. If only these were painted red they would be less hurtful. The market of Fort de Kock, of which we had heard much, was displeasing by reason of the tin roofs over all the stalls and sheds where should have been the lovely thatch of the native, or the smiling red tiles of Holland.

18

All through our roaming in Sumatra we suffered from this scar on the country's charm. Is not beauty also worthy of her hire, and shall a land be blemished because ugliness is cheap ?

We could now see Lake Manindjau like a blue jewel, like a heart of azure deep down among the hills. We descended the steep way of the mountain side to reach it. That was a wonderful walk ! The booming note of the male ape sounded in the jungle, answered by the shrill call of their mates, whilst up the steep path women swayed under burdens, their dark blue garments falling seamless from their throats. They walked proudly ; they were tall. Later in our journey I found the meaning of their steady gaze and assured gait. On that day of the walk to the lake, I but wondered at it, for I did not know of their matriarchal laws. At last, trembling with the strain of the descent, we reached a little village by the water and were faced by European chairs placed in the centre of the road for our reception. The headman of the village, booted and coated in European fashion, greeted us, telling the Assistant Resident that the fishing we wished to see had been arranged.

A macaque ape, on a chain, gave us a most practical welcome, for as soon as the alarming Boffles and interested Caddy had been hidden from his terrified round eyes, he climbed a coconut palm. After examining the nuts, the ripe ones gold, the unripe green, he screwed off a young fruit to freshen us with its water. His own master was not there, and the unfamiliar commands of the man below distressed him. Yet he did his work intelligently, and I felt we owed him a grace for the refreshing nuts he showered upon us. These nuts were as big as a child's head and full of food and drink. The coconut is the bounty of the tropics.

We were disappointed by the lake, for we had heard that it was beautiful, a peer of the lakes of Italy. Its turquoise waters and hills of jungle could not, for all their charm, be compared to the varied grandeurs of the European lakes and mountains.

In softly gliding canoes we joined the fishermen, whose boats formed a line across an angle of the water. Each craft was connected with the next by a line from which pendulous white leaves threw reflections on the water. The fishes, seeing the ghostly banners above them, swam in alarm to the margin of the lake.

Slowly the canoes followed the fugitives to the shallow water where the lotus flowers blossomed. The canoes neared each other and advanced towards a circle of stakes with matting fastened to them. Gradually men in the water narrowed the stakes, making the ring smaller, until they drew up the netting below to find a very few fish imprisoned in its meshes. A fish, not unlike a perch, had been caught, and this, for all the hours we spent on the waters, was the only gift the lake vouchsafed to us.

Caddy looked like some fairy transformed to canine shape, for I had dressed him in cool water leaves to save him from the pouring sun rays.

Afterwards, with natives who had casting-nets, we caught more fish, and cooking it beneath the mango trees, we ate it on the shore of the lake.

CHAPTER VII

A SUMATRAN ENTERTAINMENT

" We live in herds ; our joy must be collective, and
collectively we must turn to those men in whom joy is
strongest, those men who have the art to share their joy
with us."

J. CANNAN.

ON a morning there came many who had been summoned to show us their native games and songs, and
they stood grouped in the excessive sun whilst we
watched them from the verandah of the bungalow.
The men (no women came) were dressed in their true
old-world clothes. They wore baggy trousers and
blue jackets trimmed on the shoulders and down one
side with silk-woven braid. Two of the men had
brilliant jackets of coloured tissue with golden bands.
The musicians, squatting in a row on the ground,
played gongs, drawing out full rounded notes. Others
blew on reeds, woefully out of tune.

First the men " fought." This combat is a skilful
and ceremonious action rather than an onslaught
prompted by passionate affairs, or undertaken revengefully. Two men approached each other with a
curious double-jointed motion of the hand, and they
parried and bent and kicked.

They had weapons, short knives that came into play.

The puzzling duel continued till one of the men was thrown or became tired. To our amusement, this latter state suddenly overwhelmed one of the combatants. Every action was so graceful and easy that there appeared to be no violence in the overthrow, or any possible cause for fatigue.

There was also a dance of six men, who moved in circles and trod slow measures, and that was followed by the singing of an old man, who moved puppets to illustrate his lays, primitive little dolls of rag. He did not see the absurdity of his mumming, but grew tragic over the linen marionettes. Somehow, I also was affected by the recitation of their woes. He sang a lullaby, whilst another man played a piping reed which denoted the infant's cry. The old man soothed the rag figure and promised it all delights, food, flowers and gems, the very earth if it would cease to cry. The audience laughed with delight.

I could not put into English the spirit of the song, its paternity was too pastoral and patient, too tender for the cradle song of a western father.

The recitative following this one was also of a different realm of thought to ours. There lay the same rag doll, but transformed by imagery now into the semblance of a man. His clamouring son and two women were further supposed to be at the side of the recumbent figure; the wife and the other woman. The man's wife had shot him dead lest he should weaken to the younger ' other woman.'

The curious refrain of the song was always the mockery of the wife, taunting the passionate woman, she whose desires for the man, now dead, had caused the tragedy. There was no sorrow on the wife's part, or repentance, only laughter and mocking at her who had " not had her wish." At last the wife left the corpse and her heart seemed light, but the younger woman died by the side of the murdered man.

That which I had wished to see when travelling in the East two years before this present wandering, we now saw at Manindjau, a person suffering from " latah." Our hostess told me that her nurse was thus afflicted. Anxiously we warned her of the danger of such a responsible servant being thus affected, for we had heard a terrible story of a child's death which was due to a latah nurse.[1] She said it was not a serious weakness with this woman, and we entreated her to allow the nurse to be put into this nervous state.

He who suffers from latah needs only a slight shock to throw him off his mental balance. For a few moments he will act as he is commanded, or will imitate exactly the doings of the person who has caused the sudden excitement. The state is a nervous one, not actually hypnotic. It is prevalent among Malays, and, I have heard, is not unknown in Japan.

This nurse was told whilst we were dining that she was wanted. She came into the room, surprised at being sent for at that hour. The man-servant had been ordered to frighten her, and as she entered he suddenly stamped on the floor and shouted at her. At that her face quivered, her will weakened; she no

[1] Told in my last book, *Pilgrim to the Isles of Penance.*

longer owned herself. He pointed to the clock, she did likewise ; he danced, she danced too, and so for a few minutes pantomime reigned. Then she was allowed to leave the room and next day she remembered nothing, though she thought she had been " latah," for the servants teased her. A small present soothed her injured feelings.

CHAPTER VIII

ACROSS THE EQUATOR

" I have a little shadow that goes in and out with me,
And what can be the use of him is more than I can see.
He is very, very like me, from the heels up to the head."
R. L. STEVENSON.

IMAGINE your life, if you can, freed of yourself, your attributes, your importance, duties, responsibilities and the ten thousand manacles, shackles and objects which form your frame in Europe, without which, in the West, you would indeed be aimless and sad. Fling them off, as we do in our travels, when we wander like disembodied spirits loosed from possessions. Thus you have the essence of childhood consciously enjoyed. Perhaps loving these early-day countries is a throwback of the soul, or else a mental atavism, and the pleasure of living as savages, as we did later on, is merely the rather futile joy of reviving old memories of one's own primitive past in some long-ago incarnation. More probably it is the echo of the pleasures felt in remote days by ancestors who lived in an untutored age. Someone once suggested this to me, and said that so living is as foolish as to closet oneself in a nursery—a waste of time, a retracing of steps. I love children and savages, and even though

25

I have passed the stage at which they are, I still, at times, have yearnings for that state.

Talbot had easily persuaded the natives to lend us a house in the village, whither we first drove after leaving the train at Pajakombo on the second day of our progress across Sumatra. I remember the joyous feeling of rising early from the camp bed, folding it up, and eating a handful of something, I forget what, before starting to walk in the jungle. It was good to feel that there would be nothing but walking for me that day—sunshine, cries of monkeys, and beauty everywhere. No people anywhere for miles save " himself," who is to me hardly a person, but more like a presence, such as air or the sun. How the apes laughed and laughed in the trees!—some of them with a wicked, Kundry-like laugh, others in all innocence.

We saw a road being built. Here was a road in the making, still half in the mind, as much a thought as a fact; a road we waded in almost knee-deep, a road about which the Javanese overseer was in difficulties, and he consulted Talbot as we passed. Brown natives were working on it, compelled to give many days a year to it without food or money being bestowed in exchange. This is their most detested tax, their forced contribution to a civilization which they have not sought. Yet it will make life easier for them, and already does so. The weaker people go unafraid of the stronger ones, travel securely, have larger areas within their reach, and it is perhaps sentimental to pity them for having to toil at the roads. It seems, however, a heavy tax to impose, if it be considered that, counting the time they have to give to night-watchman service, and the payments made in other taxes, the total amount in works is about twelve per cent. on their annual income, though the actual money tax did not amount to more than about two per cent.[1]   These are the figures a Dutch merchant gave me.   He had been many years in Sumatra, but may have over-estimated the value of the Sumatran peasant's time.   I do not know.

Sometimes we rode, and Talbot's feet were only three inches off the path on either side of the pony. We had to cross an unfinished bridge, so we blind-folded my pony.   Then on and on we went till three o'clock in the afternoon, when, passing through the hills and jungle, we arrived at last at the Rest House on Kotabaru.   On the way we had paused for a few minutes on the very line of the Equator, and lost our faithful shadows.   I felt quite naked and lonely with-out mine.   Travelling in these bright climes a shadow follows strong and close, growing from short to long, like one's own child; suddenly to vanish and at mid-day, this seemed alarming.

In the evening we walked by the horned houses and saw the market place, but no women in this village sold at the stalls.   Here at last I learned of the power of the women in this land, and so, after long wanderings, understood the reason of that proud aspect which had first surprised me by the Lake Manindjau.

The social system of the highlands of Sumatra is matriarchal.   The House, or family, is founded on the

[1] I speak of the West Coast of Sumatra in 1911.

woman; it carries great weight, and is of far-reaching importance. When a woman marries she continues to live in the horned dwelling of her fore-mothers, which home is then added to and throws out yet another horn. Her husband but visits her, taking his sleeping mat with him. A certain responsibility rests on the eldest brother of a woman who is the Head of her House, for he must answer for the evil doings of every member of the clan, even if the delinquent be in another district.

This eldest brother is called the " Mamak," and is in command of the members of his sister's house. On him, therefore, falls the burden of everything that may go amiss in the family, for following the old native custom, or " Adat," the Dutch government holds him responsible for his tribe. Should one member of a House fall into debt, the burden of repayment falls on all its members, but it is no theft if a member of one House takes goods from another of the same clan.

There are penalties for adultery, but in the matriarchal parts of Sumatra marriages are easily broken.

In these highlands a man's children are not his heirs, for he is bound to leave his possessions to the children of his eldest sister. His nephews and nieces are therefore his " Kanemakan "—those who inherit.

In these days of easier travel it is just conceivable that should a man grow rich and leave his district his wife might go with him, but this would be unusual and not in accordance with the traditions of these people.

The women of Sumatra do not trade, but they work on the land they own. Honoured and endowed, they live in their noble dwellings beneath the traditional horn of the Victorious Buffalo.

CHAPTER IX

THE KAMPAR KANAN

" Tout est miracle."
PASCAL.

WE were to canoe down the river Kampar Kanan, a journey of four days, starting from near Kotabaru. At the town of Pakanbaru, we should join the Siak river, on which steamers ply to the north-western ports.

Our starting was delayed by a man having to return to the Rest House for my hat, which Talbot noticed I was not wearing. It was vital that I should have it, my only hat ! I was to wear it throughout fourteen weeks of blazing sunshine. In the meantime we had boarded the canoe, creeping to our places. We found that we should have to lie flat on our backs, a torturing position and horrible. The straw-plaited awning was so low we could not sit up. All day long the scenery would be hidden from us, and, with the dogs as an added inconvenience, the arrangement was almost unbearable.

Talbot resisted the roofing strongly, the Dutch Comptroller insisting the while that its withdrawal would ruin the canoe and expose us to intolerable heat. At last, with some temper lost, the offending cover was removed.

For five hours we passed between great hills which rose before us up the river's bend—walls of splendour. Here and there were clearings in the jungle made by the fires of the natives. They had grown roots or tobacco in the bared places, and moved on elsewhere when they had done their harvesting. The burnt trees stood amongst the green ones like pale ghosts, like wraiths haunting the quick. Further on, unexpected columns of the red teak flamed up suddenly from a waste of green.

A shining metal telegraph line, hung from pole to pole, ran often by the margin of the water. It seemed the filament of the white man's brain, spun even in this primal land.

Abraham, in delightful clothing, sat at one end of the canoe, and, cramped with the dogs, we took our little ease at the other end. A native behind us steered the craft; between us and Abraham two others laboured at the paddles.

For the first time in my life I felt the excitement of taking rapids. Under the firm direction of the elder oarsman we passed over many. In one place we circled in foam and rush of eddies for some six long-drawn minutes, our canoe the toy of the current.

Feeling a strange pleasure, as I surreptitiously held Talbot's coat, I asked, "What is the psychology of the love of danger?" Talbot, who loves it so well, told me it was the feeling of power over circumstances and self, the knowledge of calm where tumult might be, and of mastery over incidents that strive for empire. I could but agree, and thought that perhaps joy also lies in the unusual taste that danger gives to living, for in the West, in civilisation, life is so combed and petted, so removed from poignancy and risk, so valued, so immune, that even the possibility of dissolution seems infinitely remote. To take one's life in one's hands, to feel how thin a thread holds it from final rupture, that is a savage pleasure.

At evening we reached Pulau Gadang.

There, in glow of hibiscus and allamanda, we ate a sparse meal of rice and eggs, the only meal of the day, and finally slept on our unsheeted camp beds, with leather cushions underneath our heads and the starry host of heaven above us.

Another day of canoeing dawned, a day of trees in place of hills. On the generous branches, where orchids had their being, I saw a host of my beloved cymbidiums blossoming in the green density high above us. Grey monkeys chattered and swayed in the branches, and the apes, when they saw us, screamed with mischief and anger, throwing down stones and twigs to strike us. Some of the green giants had their trunks draped with creepers, others stood white-stemmed and solitary, striking among the tangle a clear clarion note, a solo amid the accompaniment of the rest.

Tarantang, lying on a sudden plain, greeted us at last. Stiff with long sitting, we sought the Rest House and found a mere shed, without any furniture.

The Resident was friendly to us and helped us to buy tinned foods. He lent us jugs and glasses and fed us in his house. His wife, appearing in a native sarong and jacket, also gave us kindly greeting.

We found that owing to misdirections we had passed the best tiger country, where a man-eating tiger had a price upon his head. To retrace our way up river and inland would have meant weeks of travel. There was scant hope of finding tiger further on, unless we cared to risk a long delay for an uncertain result.

The Resident of Tarantang gave us interesting information about the matriarchal people of this part of Sumatra. He had a great admiration for them, and spoke with emotion of their happy simple lives. During the three years of his administration he had dealt with only three crimes, and this in a district containing 40,000 people. In the towns, where the nationalities are mixed, men are less innocent; but here the people were governed by the matriarchal " adat," already explained.

In the evening of our coming we saw a green snake in the grass, a crocodile that lay on the bank opposite, and a wild pig that came to drink of the river just as the night was falling.

A day or two later we left the Rest House, which, in spite of the efforts of the kind administrator, was not at all a place of repose, then we again spun the web of our wandering down the river. We had now another canoe, and the country here was quite flat. We paused, at midday, in a place where a lively market was being held, and where picturesque groups of peasants viewed us with solemn surprise.

In a little boat moored to the shore we found a deer

no bigger than a hare, a beautifully formed animal which had been trapped in the thickets by a Sumatran. We bought it from him, and when at evening we reached Bangkinang, I was taught how to cook it. A whole haunch fell to my share.

The river was greatly swollen. At Bangkinang the steps of the Rest House were covered with water, and the verandah floor was only just above the level of its increasing volume. The river had risen some twenty feet in two days, but thinking that there would soon be a decrease in the floods we took up our abode in the Rest House. Of Bangkinang, I remember only ibises and orchids—ibises that rested on a log by the river, and pigeon orchids, Dendrobium and Crumenatum, that flowered along a dark stem above them. The flowers lived a single scented day and at evening died. They were so alike that only a magic word, which somehow stayed unspoken, seemed needed to change bird to flower and flower to very bird. The ibis had more days to fly in the sun; the orchid had its untellably sweet scent whilst it hung above the water, wherein fell bees drunken with its honey.

That was Bangkinang.

From Taratak Boeloeh to Pakan Baru was an immense walk in the torturing sun. It was there that we boarded the steamer.

Labuan Bilik had courteous people, clothed in gorgeous woven sarongs. At Tanjong Baley lived a Rajah; after these places came Delli and Medan.

DENDROBIUM CRUMENATUM.   THE PIGEON ORCHID.

To face page 34.

CHAPTER X

MEDAN

"God made the country, and man made the town," quoted one. "A great argument in favour of man," replied a Londoner.

FROM Medan, the chief town of the East of Sumatra, we proposed recrossing Sumatra, having the harbour of Siboga on the north-west coast as ultimate destination, and Toba Meer, the heart of the Batak region, as pausing place on our way.

Medan seemed a veritable Europe after the hungry lands we had been through. Fresh butter was a revolution in our lives, and good cooking an epoch in our travels.

Abraham, in honour of civilisation, was dressed more beautifully than ever, with fresh white jackets and painted blue and brown sarongs, with starched cloths for his head twisted behind into bows like wings. In consequence of this display he wrote us piteous notes saying he had nothing to eat because he had spent all his money on clothes ; he begged that we would advance him money, which we did. He enjoyed writing, and was proud of using the European alphabet.

We spent the day in buying provisions of tea, tinned meats, and tinned fruits in readiness for our journey to the Batak Land, to the Lake of Toba Meer.

35

We could have gone some of the way in a motor car, but this would have been uncomfortable, uninteresting, and very expensive, so we decided to travel by rail, carriage and foot.

Our first stage was from Medan to Siantar, three hours of which we did in a leisurely train, which had almost run the full length of its course when it left us at Tebingting. There we took four carriages. Had Boffles been with us we should have needed a fifth. We had, however, sent him and Caddy back to England, mainly because they would not eat rice, and we had but little else to give them. Each carriage was only a sedan chair, with a miniature pony to draw it, and a Cingalese driver sitting on one shaft—the sort of vehicle a Sumatran fairy godmother might produce from a pumpkin for the benefit of a dark-skinned Cinderella. A sullen and unpleasant Comptroller was induced to make the drivers, who were under his jurisdiction, lower their Barabbaselian charges ; he enjoyed sitting in judgment on Chinese and Indian coolies, but seemed unwilling to prevent misdeeds being committed on the unhappy traveller.

At last we started, with grumbling on all sides.

For forty miles we drove along a dusty highway towards Siantar, past tobacco plantations and past towering trees which had been burnt and mangled by planters white and brown. Here and there kindly creepers covered the scarred trees which lifted leafless trunks towards the sun, splendid Samsons mighty in their affliction.

For nine hours next day we walked and drove

through burnt country, country under the cultivation of both native and white men. Up and down we travelled through the plains and hills, thick with long grasses and quite treeless here, till at last we stood above Toba Meer. We had reached the Batak Land.

CHAPTER XI

THE BATAKS

"I have said the Bataks are not bad people, and I think so, notwithstanding they eat one another, and relish the flesh of a man better than that of an ox or pig. You must merely consider that I am giving you an account of a novel state of society. The Bataks are not savages, for they write and read, and think full as much and more than those who are brought up at our Lancastrian and National schools."

Memoirs of Sir T. S. Raffles.

OUR days among the Bataks were as no others for interest, crowded with wonder ; we seemed to live in another planet.

I am impatient to record the most coloured incidents, but I must touch on the drab ones as I pass.

Our first knowledge of the Bataks was tiresome, European, conventional. They murmured against the payment we promised them for taking our boxes down to the lake side, and they took part against us with the Cingalese drivers who wished to overcharge us in spite of their written contract. We left the discontented ones, and after standing on the hills above the blue-orbed lake, we descended to Toba Meer, passing through plantations of maize.

We saw the Bataks working in the fields, clothed in long blue stuffs, dark coloured, woven into ample garments which were draped about them.

Next day we went on to the island of Samosir in the steam launch, which the Resident at Medan had promised should be at our disposal for as long as we might desire it.

The Bataks in the boat were Christians; they wore German cotton pyjama suits, and sang hymns in their own language to European tunes. They troubled me. I heard later they had German and evangelical names, that there was one who had been christened Bismarck, and another Luther, for nearly all the missionaries in the Dutch Indies are Germans.

I have no desire for the Batak people to be pagans; I do not want them to be cannibals as they were when Raffles came here some hundred years ago, but I feel that if one travels ten thousand miles or more, it is to see and learn, and understand something different from what is at home, something strange and new.

Mynheer Mittendorf, the Dutch Comptroller, met us at the quay. He bade us welcome to the Rest House where he was living, no official residency or house having as yet been built.

Some kindly mental sprite suggested to me that it would be well to ascertain if there was any charge for the launch which had been lent to us on behalf of the Government. Talbot asked the man in charge and, to his intense amazement, was asked to pay a pound an hour for the craft. As we carried but small sums of money upon us, the unforeseen levy meant that we were money-bound on the island of Samosir instead of cruising about for many days as had been our intention.

Mynheer Mittendorf became our friend and companion. Having lately come from Europe he was still Western in his ways ; young, eager and interested. He did not sleep from noon till four o'clock in the afternoon as do nearly all his compatriots, neither did he dress by day in native clothes or in European pyjamas, like the majority of the officials.

We kept a joint household with Mynheer Mittendorf, giving each other lunches and dinners, and keeping strangely varying hours for these repasts. In his garden were roses and lilies. On Saturday we filled our house and the long verandah with flowers in celebration of the coming Sunday.

Every day we fed the fat gold fish in the little garden pond. So enormous were these fish that the young ducks could stand upon them ; they used them as platforms to raise themselves towards the bread we threw them ; for Mittendorf's Christian boy baked bread. Of our first day among the Bataks I still have much to tell.

CHAPTER XII

A BATAK TRIAL

> " Moreover, with regard to any sinful conduct, it is not
> the act itself, but the sinful intention by which one incurs
> guilt. It is only when the heart co-operates with the bodily
> members in the commission of an offence that guilt is
> incurred. The essential thing in all conduct is the inten-
> tion of the heart."
>
> RABBI BACHYE.

WE had broken our fast and were looking at some
books, dear links with Europe, when the verandah in
front of the large dining-room was transformed into a
square of human drama, and Mynheer Mittendorf sat
in judgment upon several tragic cases. Around the
verandah on a hard seat were many Rajahs, the Batak
heads of the villages, but as the time passed they
slipped off the benches on to the floor and sat with those
whom they judged.

The outer man of the Bataks is tremendously
ugly. These Rajahs, though rather superior in looks
to the common people, were of a very low type. They
varied strangely in colour. Some were almost black,
others very brown. The lower garment of the Chiefs
was of the native blue home-spun material, the upper
garment an official European jacket, completed by a
small blue hat with a gold or silver band, which

to them was dearer than any crown could be. These bands, presented to them by the Dutch Government with the rest of the page-boy uniform, show their rank, the gold braid adorning the higher, the silver the lesser rulers. There are twenty-five gold Rajahs in Samosir, all of whom are pensioned by the Dutch at a generous and increasing rate. From them no labour is exacted, though upon them falls the obligation of collecting the taxes from the lesser people. Their pensions compensate them in part for the loss of their slaves, now mostly freed.

Among the people acting as witnesses were women who sat upon the floor swathed in blue garments, the unmarried girls naked to below the breasts, the married ones clothed with drapery that fell from the neck. Sitting amongst them was the chief offender of them all, a man undergoing trial for murder. He seemed to be in a stupor, bowed and numbed. He bent round, ape-like eyes upon the floor and seldom lifted them. When he did raise them, dull wonder showed therein. His fingers were very short, his thumbs long like the useful toes of the monkey; he seemed but to have half shaken free of the state of the beast; the trammels of the primitive were not removed from him. Man—" the fairy prince " of children's tales— had not, in spirit, leapt up from out of the form of the animal.

I pitied him. He could never catch up to this era in development. He was behind even his own people, the Bataks. His life had fallen on a day of demands greater than he was able to meet.

For months he had thus sat hearing his people witnessing against him. To-day, the slow trial had ended—he was condemned.

The remnant of a frog was brought in, attached to a stick, only its leg was left. The rest had gone to dust. Over it the solemn oaths were uttered, the terrible doom invoked. " As the frog is dust, as nothing of it remains but a fragment, so may I be crushed, killed and broken asunder if my oaths are lies." With words of this kind the witnesses branded their testimony as true.

The Rajahs talked together, gave Mynheer Mittendorf their judgment, advised that the murderer should suffer twenty years' imprisonment, and Mynheer concurred and pronounced the sentence. Then the man was led away. He had stoned a woman, a married woman, somewhere in a field outside her village. She was missed at the evening meal; the next day she was found dead. Perhaps he had been jealous of her, perhaps she had refused to commit adultery.

Not many years ago he would have been tied to a post and have been speared to death, or, were he judged guilty of adultery, he would have been eaten, living, by those whom he had wronged—not passionately or revengefully killed, but according to fixed rules in the Batak book of the Laws of Punitive Feasts. The woman's husband [1] and her brother would first have

[1] This is according to Raffles. The only cannibalism the Batak Chiefs told us of was the sacrificial eating of men, with which the following chapter deals.

eaten of him, and then, until he was dead, the men of the village would have fed upon him, but the women were forbidden to take part in the ghastly act.

Formerly a woman taken in adultery had her feet tied together and bamboos were bound to the outer part of the ankles, the further ends of the bamboo being bent over into the earth. At a signal the ankle cords were cut and the bamboos, thereby attached to her, released from the tension, would spring up against her, sharp as swords, and kill her.

The ape-like man of murderous stones was sent, I think, to Java, where he would labour all his life, suffer home-sickness in the consuming way of primitive people whose whole life is bounded by their village ; he would, at last, become rooted in the new life and finally sink into the sort of despairing content of caged animals.

The hearing of his crime was now succeeded by two other curious cases. A woman, dark and evil-eyed, with lips distorted and discoloured by betel chewing, sat on the floor, and behind her was her husband. He wore round his head a reed bound as a fillet—sure sign, Talbot told me, of headache or mental distress in primitive people. His face was as that of a Cyclops. The woman asked for divorce ; she had been married for a year, and she swore that her husband beat her and had once attempted to cut her throat. She had, however, cost much money—110 guilders, I think—so she could not easily be freed. A wise judgment was given, the Chiefs deciding that she must return to her village, the Rajah of which would watch her case.

Should he deem she had cause for grief, she would be loosed from the yoke of marriage.

After this case another woman clamoured for divorce. For three months she had been married, against her will, so she said, for as a slave she was sold for 100 guilders to her husband. That man looked a poor, humbled individual, who shrank under his hand-plaited straw cap, and seemed to fear his furious purchase and consort. Her former master was there as witness, and he and the Rajah swore that she had been willing enough to marry. Then from the little crowd of people came a man who said he was her father. He offered to buy her for fifty rupees, because, as a parent, he should be allowed to have her for this low price. All the Bataks laughed aloud at his words, for, they said, " Her parents never were known. This man wishes to possess her ; he is no father." The amused Rajahs decreed the same fate for her as for her sister in discontent. So both went back to their village, and the Court rose.

CHAPTER XIII

CANNIBALISM

" Mann ist was er iszt."

ONE day, through all the cool yet golden hours of the sun's shining, we sat in our verandah. Chiefs came and visited us ; to them we spoke through an interpreter, asking them many things.

The Rajah in my picture was the cleverest of them all. Talbot taught him to look through his telescope, which he quickly learned to do, laughing loud and long with bursting sides and noisy delight at whatever it was he saw away in a far field near a village. It is curious how quickly aboriginal people learn to use a telescope.

The Esquimaux to whom Talbot took cheap small telescopes could see through them almost as well as he could through his very superior glass—this, though he is as expert with his glass as any Highland stalker.

The humbler Bataks would not spy through the strange instrument and an old man came and led them away.

According to Batak belief, so the Chiefs said, man has a supreme soul which descends from God and

46

inhabits the human body during life, but at death returns to its Divine source.

Beside this somewhat abstract and transcendental soul, this people believes that man contains a spirit which even after his death imbues his body with qualities. " Let us eat a man's flesh," they cried, " that we may possess his mettle, his courage, the luck that was his." The attributes dear to the Batak mind would thus be found equally in the enemy, or even in the criminal, for it was the life force and the vim which they most sought in their grim feasts. Raffles, in letters to a friend, wrote that old people were set amongst the branches of trees, whilst the younger inhabitants of the villages danced about, shaking the branches and singing, " The fruit is ripe—the fruit is ripe." When the victims fell exhausted to the ground they were eaten by the young men.

Our chief would not admit that even the detested Pak-Paks had ever done this thing. Even if the Bataks ate their parents it is probable that they awaited their natural death.

The Europeans whom we met who had any acquaintance with this people seemed to think that the sacrificial eating of parents had never been practised. Since, however, by means of cannibalism, the Bataks hoped to obtain the qualities of the enemy, how much more must they have desired to perpetuate in themselves the personalities of their elders ? We, therefore, concluded that probably the flesh of parents was eaten, though it is also possible that the Bataks had other means of preserving the mettle of their own immediate dead. It is only lately that Dutch legislation has compelled these natives to bury their dead. They used to keep the corpses for days under their houses until, at the final rites, they drained the decaying body by means of bamboos, which carried the liquid parts away into the ground. The remnants of the departed were then placed in large stone boxes, which were kept in the villages close to the houses.

A Military Comptroller whom we had met elsewhere in Sumatra, and who had had charge of Samosir some eight years before, told us that the Chiefs assured him that their reason for eating their enemies was that they should be utterly obliterated.[1] This was a fearful vengeance wreaked upon detested foes, a horrible consummation visited upon the loathed oppressors.

The Bataks ate and still eat horse flesh, yet " meat-hunger " may have been one of the reasons of their cannibalism ; its main purpose was punitive and ethical. Their belief in the merit of man-eating was, perhaps, strengthened by their enjoyment of it. Several of them told me that the hand is the most delicious part. " Like bears' paws," Talbot mused, " which look like human hands when served at dinner in Russia and taste excellent."

At last the chief went back to his village and we with him. We saw that what looked like gardens, walled in, were in reality hamlets screened with bamboos, most lovely sentinels of these villages. From

[1] Compare the punishment that Pomponia meted out to Philologus, betrayer of Cicero. She "made him cut off his own flesh by pieces, and roast and eat it."—PLUTARCH.

four to six houses formed a village, and opposite each house was a rice-house. Round about the dwelling was a low mud rampart, and within it a thick high wall of bamboos through which an enemy could hardly pass, for whilst he was trying to force an entrance those within opposed him.

Some years ago there was war, always war; not fierce, devastating battles, but petty raids, robbery of cattle and of fishing nets, the feeble hostility of one " marga " for another.

A marga is somewhat like a clan; it is the family of a Rajah. Each village has a Rajah, and there are also more powerful Rajahs who protect several villages. The social system of the Bataks rests on patriarchal foundations. A man when asked how many children he has tells only of his boys—his daughters are not counted among the number of his offspring. The woman keeps her name, but the husband, when a son is born, changes his in this manner :

The man's name we will say is " Baerdjoe," and he has a son who is named " Si Bane "; then Baerdjoe becomes " Ama Si Bane," which is, the father of Bane ; and even the grandfather changes also and is known as " Ompol Bane."

Then there is another division into which the people fall, and this is one which has puzzled some learned Europeans and which has, I think, been wrongly explained in at least one Dutch report on the Bataks. This is the " Bioes." A Bioes seems to be a kind of sect, or number of people sharing one variation of worship.

There is a mountain of Toba Meer called the Poesoek Boehit, or the Head with the Little Hair. A few trees at the summit give this appearance, and some of the people worship here once a year and are of its Bioes. This place is possessed of a spirit, which is the reason of its being worshipped. The worship is always for a place and not for an animal or for a person, otherwise a Bioes would more closely resemble totemic worship than it appears to do.

We left our Rajah for a while, agreeing to return to see the people of his village dancing in the moonlight whilst one of them invoked an oracle.

. . . .

At dinner, that evening, we had evidence that a Batak's thirst for revenge is best slaked by the devouring of the offender. A man ran in excitedly crying : " A child has been bitten by a mad dog in the village of ——." " I should like," said Mynheer Mittendorf, " to see the dog, for if it is mad the child must go to Java for Pasteur treatment." " The dog cannot be brought," said the Batak with hesitation—" Why not ? " " Because the child's parents have already eaten the dog."

CHAPTER XIV

THE MAGIC DANCE

" Leave us, we have good customs and are without sin."
(Batak Chief's words to German Missionary.)

THE women had left their looms in the rice house and sat no longer, picturesque, and busy, weaving the blue garments of the people. The pots they had borne on their heads from the lake side were full of green herbs and lake water, wherefrom would be compounded the fine blue dye of the Bataks, whilst the nauseous smell of the mixture filled all the village.

The sun had set, the moon had risen, the dance might now be held. These dances originate from the Hindus, who must, it is almost certain, have influenced even the Bataks. The movements of the dancers are confined mostly to the slow waving of their hands and snake-like movements of the arms.

" Good dances for hot climates," remarked Talbot; and this is true of all the dancing of these Isles of Java and Sumatra.

From among the men there came one who, bowing, approached a staff stuck into the ground, a staff with a man's head carved on it, and within which were the ashes of a child. A child, killed perhaps by burning cinders being thrust into its mouth and throat, for in the dust of what once was the heart of the infant resides the strength of its spirit.

Wooden clarionets, gongs from China, mellow, beautiful drums and rude pipes accompanied the dancer till he held up his hand to hear the oracle speak. Then the message was given to those about him, trivial it seemed to me, but to them it was vital, for the coming or withholding of rain means food, or else hunger. The foaling of a mare is a great gain where there are so few possessions. The lives of these people are bounded by narrow horizons.

In a few years' time the Bataks of Toba Meer will, I think, be Christians. Some are becoming Mahommedan, but the German missionaries have the greater influence. Already the people are half ashamed of their dances, their fathers' ways and thoughts.

The Christian Bataks, of whom we saw but little, send out teachers to the further isles, and these instruct the natives, under the aegis of the resident German missionaries. I believe the converts even contribute to the payment of these teachers. Nowhere, however, does the new faith break on the people with a dazzling dayspring such as inspired the early European believers. I should like the preachers to go about like fires, burning up the old dross and lighting all the good there is in their ancient faith. Thus would Christianity bring increase into their lives.

Instead, the missionaries, many of them most devout men, show the converts their vibrating facet of Christian truth as emanating from a book, sandwiched between arithmetic and geography in the schools, and

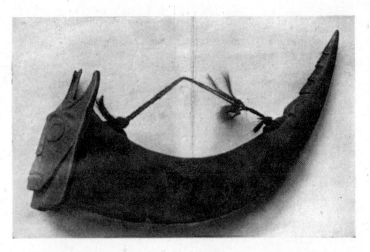

HORN TO BE CARRIED INTO BATTLE. IT CONTAINS THE HEART OF AN
ENEMY.

OUR BATAK BOOK.

To face page 52.

give it to the people along with cotton pyjamas and European ideas.

What a drab world it will be when our great grand-children come to it ! The levelling of education will have killed the beauty of rustic language and weakened original thought, the levelling of class will have killed individuality and have wilted the life of art. The westernising of the world will have withered the picturesque, the great wild animals will have been killed out, the naked will be clothed in ugliness. My heart turns sick to think of it. But generations hence these far people will have, perhaps, a civilization of their own, and having passed through the dull period of western imitation, will find individual art and thoughts. So ever and again the earth will be renewed.

CHAPTER XV

THE BATAK LANGUAGE

"Man, God, the World, every one in their kind bear
some fruits. All things have their proper time to bear."
MARCUS AURELIUS.

THE most extraordinary fact about the Bataks, and one
which sets them apart from all the other peoples of the
world, is that they are not mere cannibals but that they
are literary cannibals. They have not taken their
alphabet from the Arabic as have the Malays, but have
evolved one for themselves, though it is almost
certainly derived from some Indian system and is in
some ways like Sanskrit writing.

The Batak alphabet consists of nineteen letters, which
vary slightly in the three or four dialects into which the
language is diverted.

Their system of writing is syllabic. The Bataks
have a large range of words, and their language contains at least seven thousand or eight thousand words,
not including the derivations. The written idiom is
very much simpler than Sanskrit.

The books of the Bataks date back some eight
generations. Whether this people has added to its
literature during recent years I do not know. I think
not.

The characters are written, or painted, on the folded bark of a tree, and the precious volumes belong not to individuals but to whole villages. When we were seeking a Batak book, the old chief from whom we wished to buy it said he must ask permission of his village to sell it. He returned some days later with the volume, of which I show a picture. He alone could read the curious lore it contained, and he sometimes entertained the assembled villagers with its ancient teachings.

Some of the rude pages of our book contained diagrams, with figures of men and women, which showed no greater art than do the drawings of a small child. These illustrations designated the proper positions to be taken up by the people in their dances. This volume was a warrior book, but another we obtained was called *The Book of the Hen* and deals with omens. Therein is written, that if a hen be taken and its head cut off, the course of its blood must be watched, for if it flows towards the North the enemy will come from thence, or if to the South, from the South will peril come. I was given the translation of a few pages of a Batak book which is in a museum in Holland. It is to a kind and learned professor at Leyden that I owe what I know of the Batak language and writing. He told me that it is very difficult to find any part of the Batak *pustaka*, or holy writing, which can be translated, as the contents of most of the volumes are quite unintelligible, even to those who well know the Batak language. The simpler parts need lengthy commentaries and a wide knowledge of the ways of the Batak folk before they mean anything to the European reader.

These books contain much of astrology, mixed with much that is curious and with odd superstitions and futilities. Often the meaning dwindles down to mere abracadabra, rarely if ever is there any reference to the Laws of the Bataks.

The book, from which the following translation is taken, begins with a long tale about some poisonous tree growing upon the grave of a saint, who, though innocent, was killed by the crowd. The following are but a few of the instructions given by a " medicine " woman about some remedy which should act as antidote to the deadly poison of the said tree.

Translation.

" You should take the following ingredients : the roots of gingilis, the fruit of the banana, also some white, good-smelling rice, and pepper-corns.

" Then you should weigh and take four parts of gingili-oil, three parts of banana water, and mix with two parts of rice water. Then gather nine siputuri leaves, and with the mixture paint two letters of the alphabet on each leaf.

" Drop the leaves in the rest of the fluid mixture, and go to the river to bathe, using seven lemons, curcuma, and other scented fruits "—So the tale goes on with great wealth of uninteresting detail.

The Bataks will survive, I think, all the changes that are being thrust upon them. They will spring forward into the twentieth century direct from their present state, which is almost primal. They will not gradually evolve as our race has done, and whether this rapid evolution will be good for them time only can reveal.

CHAPTER XVI

FAREWELL TO THE BATAKS

"There are still other lands and countries beautiful and deep, desirable and bright and thriving."

TEACHINGS OF ZOROASTER.

CAME a day when we had to leave the Batak country, with its deep lake high among the hills. We did not go as we had come ; instead, we rowed away at dawn in a war canoe some sixty feet long. Twenty-one men went with us, nineteen to row and two to steer ; slaves at the oars, a Rajah at the bow, where was a carved and decorated column. During the ten hours on the water there was cover for us beneath a little thatch, where we crouched in some discomfort, and all the time slaves sang, slaves who in a year's time were to be freed. The bondsmen of the Bataks now share the houses of their masters, and eat with them and work with them, but they can never marry the women of the higher classes, nor can they trace their families back as the free men do.

They suffer no cruelty, but the fact of slavery must be bitter, for once when a man was killed his murderer pleaded in extenuation of his crime that " the man I killed called me slave." His Batak judges understood that death had to follow such an insult, yet the murderer was a slave.

58

There were in front of us, in the canoe, two men, small and wizened; one I called Alberich, for he looked like a dwarf of the nether world. He sang " O Liborta," and the others took up the refrain after him, but I never knew what the meaning of " O Liborta " could be.

Then also there were two I named Tweedledee and Tweedledum, who clucked " Tong tong " roundly and curiously with their tongues. To them I gave some fruit; rather bitter it was, but they found it delicious, and shared it with three other men, leaving for themselves but a fragment.

We rowed away. As the evening fell the Rajah waxed furiously excited and urged the men on with cries and with loud stamping at the bow; only the helmsmen remained mute and impassive. The efforts of the men lessened as we neared Balige; they had rowed us fifty-five miles, and unlike Western people who, as they reach their goal, put forth their best efforts, these Easterners seemed to grow faint just as their task was nearly accomplished.

We reached our journey's end. The day was lost in the sapphire spaces of the night. We made gifts to the Rajah and to the men of the canoe before it glided to its moorings. As we lost sight of it round a curve of the lake we sighed, because we had said " Good-bye" for ever to the Bataks.

CHAPTER XVII

FROM BALIGE TO SIBOGA

"Or wilt thou rather . . .
  Half-faded fiery blossoms pale with heat
  And full of bitter summer, but more sweet
  To thee than gleanings of a northern shore
  Trod by no tropic feet ? "
                                        SWINBURNE.

OF the first part of the journey, I remember only that
the country was mountainous and beautiful. Low
grass hills now surrounded us, whilst hollyhocks and
honey-suckle bedecked our way and marguerites grew
eight feet high.

I remember too, at Taroetoeng, the tree of the
" forbidden fruit," [1] for all night long its sweetness
filled the air. I saw in the morning its triple glory of
leaf, flower and fruit.

Of the second night spent in the heights amongst
trees and ferns, the memory I hold is of the coolies,
frightened, because in the jungle there are tigers. They
burned lamps by the stables lest the great animals
should come and eat the pony.

Then came a day of painful riding, and the ponies
trembled with the strain of the descent.

---

[1] Citrus Decumana, otherwise pompelmoes, or shaddock, a variety
of grape fruit.

"THE FORBIDDEN FRUIT."
Citrus Decumana.

To face page 60.

In the evening we had reached Siboga, a town of sweet scents. The Jambosa was in flower, its petunia coloured petals carpeting the ground by the Rest House.

On this journey, two Eurasian Comptrollers had shown themselves ungracious, but now as we arrived at Siboga, the wife of a Eurasian Resident invited us to her house at seven o'clock in the evening. We were tired and hungry, food having been difficult to get, as we had arrived too late to do any marketing. Hopefully we entered the house, which was filled with tawny-coloured children. Mevrouw gave us lemonade and soft words.

From the German store we collected letters and money and sailed for Nias. We raised Abraham's wages to four rupees a week to prevent his leaving us, he being afraid of the Nias people, who, we had been told, are head hunters.

CHAPTER XVIII

NIAS

"Là, tout n'est qu'ordre et beauté,
Luxe, calme et volupté."
C. BAUDELAIRE.

A BRILLIANT shore, embracing palms and cliffs and natural grottoes, with hills in the distance ; such was our farewell vision of Sumatra, whilst our ship was sailing as though it were being steered for the very orb of the sun, now low in the horizon. The magnificent goodbye of the sun to our side of the earth flashed in an almost audible sunset, which translated into sound would have been like Wagner's music. Then, suddenly, the rain blotted out the heights and the deeps, and I watched instead " the silken lady of the ship," as I named to myself a Sumatran fellow passenger travelling with her husband.

Next day was full of heat and the smarting glare of the waters, until, at four o'clock, we reached Gunung Sitoli, the port of call for Nias, where every fortnight a steamer delivers a slight mail and takes up a cargo of coconuts. No European, excepting a few officials and missionaries, ever lands. An Italian professor did attempt to gain some knowledge of Nias, but fell sick of malaria and had to leave.

We were positively the first to come to Nias seeking pleasure.

On the pier the gentle form of the Assistant Resident greeted our sight. We presented him with the letter of introduction that we had brought to him.

The Rest House, he told us, was under repair, so he led us to the Fort where there were empty rooms, which he put at our disposal.

We had brought tinned foods and cooking pans, we possessed also our camp beds, so we felt self-supporting; but when, by the light of the torches we saw the rooms in the Fort my spirits waned a little. Owing to the failure of rain there was no water, but countless ants and a great deal of dust. We praised the abode, however, saying we could quite well live there, as indeed we could have done, but Mynheer van Vuuren was kindly insistent and led us to his house. We demurred, thinking that the sight of our abode had compelled him to offer us the shelter of his roof.

On the way to his house, in a moment of caught breath, I saw the long main road of the little low-roofed town, all the buildings of which are inhabited by Chinese traders. Between the shops of the Celestials lay the white road, on either side of which— imagine the beauty of it !—grew palms like great stone columns, or like lighthouses, flashing green from their beacons. Their white and rounded trunks, massive and architectural pillars, stretched down the avenue as far as eye could see.

Even now as I write I feel an echo of the pleasure I had when we reached Mynheer van Vuuren's house.

A bed with sheets, a real dressing-table, a washing-stand—triune delights—greeted my gaze. It was long since I had enjoyed these luxuries, and I was tired and stiff from the ride from Taroetoeng. Therefore a bed with a mattress seemed the pinnacle of comfort.

We bathed, and dined to satiety. Afterwards I slept softly and whole-heartedly, murmuring lines from Baudelaire.

CHAPTER XIX

THE MISSION HOUSE

"J'ai toujours été un de ceux pour qui le monde visible existe."

BRINGING a letter from Mynheer van Vuuren, we burst unexpectedly on the lives of Herr von Erlen and his wife as they sat in their creeper-covered verandah. A neophyte was with them, a young German who was to take up mission work in Nias ; he was now being taught the Nias language. We were welcomed warmheartedly; the pleasure of European greeting European in these far climes pervaded our arrival.

We were given the young man's room (I do not know where he was bestowed), and after a bountiful *rijst tafel* we slept until the day had cooled a little. Then " home " seemed to speak aloud in the coffee and fresh milk and home-made cakes which our hostess set before us. Cows must be grazing somewhere near—delightful thought !

How eminently comfortable, how " gemütlich " was everything here after the unhomely ways of the Dutch colonists.

Apart from this heroic home-life—for to bake cakes in that climate, and, in spite of native Christian servants, to preserve a home in Nias is heroic—there was a remarkable, and it seemed to us, a forced gaiety in this Mission House. A camaraderie with the natives stretched to the point of absurdity.

An old chief came who wished to sit on the floor in his natural way, but a chair was insistently offered to him, and the clothed and booted old fellow, after shaking hands with us, accepted the European seat.

The natives of Nias are intensely aristocratic in their customs and laws, and though they are without the ceremony and servility of the kingdoms of Java, they would be quite prepared to treat the white man as a ruler, which indeed he is.

The missionaries make of the native a spoilt brother, and by destroying his ideals before thoroughly imbuing him with their own, they turn him into a hopeless bastard, fathered of no tradition.

After coffee we went out, walking along a " pig path," as the narrow walks are called by the people of Nias, whose highways they used to be. From this track we came to the broad road of the colonists, which had been made by native labour without payment, in the same way as the roads of Sumatra.

The Niasers detest this burden and see no possible use for the highway which, indeed, they seldom use, for there is but little communication between the villages, and there are, of course, no motors, carts or carriages, and but very few horses.

The people still walk in the ditches by the roads as though treading their ancient narrow ways, and when, at the mission station, some of them saw the picture of an aeroplane, their first exclamation was one of joy, for they thought that if once the terrible white man took to flying he would no more need roads.

Some men came furtively to Herr von Erlen as we walked, and asked : " Why have those white people come to Nias ; what are they about to do ; have they come to take our lands ? " Our host answered : " They have come to walk about," an answer that seemed near enough to the truth to be a delightful summary of our motive for travelling many thousands of miles to Nias !

Others of the people, less brave, ran to Frau von Erlen crying : " Will they hurt us ; they are so big ? " The Niasers are seldom more than some five feet three inches in height and we seemed as giants who had come among them.

The evening breeze woke up among the tall trees and dense foliage of the jungle along the hills. To the village in the valley the women returned bowed down by baskets full of green food for the pigs. In the palms birds with black and golden plumage gave back long notes to Talbot's whistled invitation.

Bats big as foxes passed us with massive movements, and a green and pink parrot like a flying flower winged its way to the jungle. In the trees are green pigeons, and once in the forest I saw glinting a copper-coloured bird which I was told was also a pigeon.

I made many efforts to obtain one of these red birds but I never succeeded. I saw them again in the islands of the Mentawi Group.

The night now spread its tail along the sky, blue peacock, argus-eyed with stars. We went back to the house embraced by creepers, before proceeding to the village where a dance was being prepared for us, for Herr von Erlen and his wife, unlike many of their Lutheran brethren, were not displeased by dancing.

We supped, and afterwards Frau von Erlen closed the shutters carefully and locked the doors. Did the grating of the key in the lock hurt her, I wondered, for this was the only bolted door in North Nias, the only house where theft need be feared. Ah! Europe was setting her seal on Nias; the people were becoming Westernized, the closing doors proclaimed the fact.

With lanterns we went down to the hamlet, and sat on logs of wood. The unbeautiful women of the village greeted us. They wore Chinese garments, and bands of gold on their heads, like crowns of ancient peoples or from out Grecian tombs; buckles and bibs of gold they had, and curling leaves of metal in their ears.

They had learnt some Western conventions; they shook hands with us. " Can one never escape Europe ? " I wondered. Then, in a wild cry, the newer continents were banished from my thoughts, for " Hu, hu, hu " called the warriors, as they approached each other from north and south with spears and shields of wood. Their cries were those of wild mankind.

They came stamping and calling, and in the houses behind us Chinese gongs gave out their booming notes.

They neared each other slowly; the men of two

villages stood before us. All who had dared came armed and in their red war jackets, below which hung loin cloths. A few were afraid to come, for the Dutch forbid the native dances, which awaken the old passions of the people.

I felt a slight tremor when I saw the wild looks leaping to their faces and heard their primal challenges. The dances had transformed them suddenly, the head-hunter and the savage stood revealed.

Afterwards the women danced alone, advancing and retreating, mouthing weird labial sounds like the utterance of early man striving for speech. As they passed they licked each other's tongues in salutation.

As we walked home, Frau von Erlen told me how much these people fear death. " It is their heathen beliefs which make their death hideous," she said. " But Christians usually far more than Pagans dread it," I reminded her. " Well, I do not wonder at their fear," she assented, "for, after all, death is very unnatural," and was surprised at my burst of laughter !

Next morning I was in the little garden of the Mission House with the lady thereof. She was watching her gardener sowing seeds in the forceful earth. He came entreating her. I asked what he had said.

" He asked me to unpin my hair and let it hang loosely about me," she said, " or else the seeds he is planting cannot grow." But she was unmoved and would not encourage such superstition. When she went indoors I let my hair down, for the fancy of the seeds being helped pleased me, and the joy of the Nias gardener when he saw me thus did, I daresay, thrill the grain he was planting to quicker life and greener health.

Soon afterwards we returned to Gunung Sitoli.

CHAPTER XX

THE HEADHUNTERS

"They walk upon the road their fathers trod.

. . . .

In wakefulness or sleep their sole desire
To keep the settled plan of things entire."

ABU'L-ALA.

WE had before us a few days at Gunung Sitoli and were
looking forward to going to Telok Dalam, the
southern port of Nias. Mynheer van Vuuren had
sent a messenger on foot to prepare the German missionary of the south for our coming. We saw much
that was strange at Gunung Sitoli. I bought myself a
golden crown in a plaited wicker basket; an old man
brought it to me shamefacedly and in secret, for crowns
and swords are things too intimate to sell.

There were in the prison next to the house of the
Resident two men, a Chief and his son, awaiting their
trial for head-hunting. It had happened thus. They
came from the centre of Nias, where the Chief had
built a new house. " And how shall we have a house
and never a ghostly slave to guard it ? " the father must
have asked, then added, " Go and get me a skull to
bury under the lintel that at least one spirit may watch
the house."

So the son went out with his special head-snatching

weapon, and, passing by the people of his father's village, he came to a field beyond the next hamlet. There a young woman was working, and humming over some plants she was gathering for the pigs to eat. The Chief's son slashed off her head from behind so that it fell laughing in its blood. The head was buried beneath the new house that the ghost of the girl might guard the home of her master. No anger was expected from her spirit, no return of evil; the soul was enslaved by the murderer, it would play its part as watcher over the dwelling. The Chief declared that there should be a great feast, and that many pigs would be killed and roasted. He would, himself, provide the bounty instead of taxing the people for it, for they were still in debt to the neighbouring villages for the swine they had eaten in honour of the funeral of the late Chief, the father of our headhunter.

The Chief's son was to be praised in song for having hallowed the new house with the girl's skull, and all night long there was to be eating, and dancing and merriment.

Now whilst the feast was being celebrated the husband of the murdered girl travelled north and brought news of these doings to the Comptroller, whereupon the Chief and his men were arrested by the Javanese soldiers sent down to Central Nias to capture them. " Are there then to be no guardians for our new houses ? " they asked. " Better that we should shelter in the ruins of the old houses. When a Chief dies, shall his spirit go alone to the distant place, and shall no others go with him ?

" Shall his body be left alone on the raised dais of wood beneath the great trees, where we leave it that it may not pollute the earth ? "

" Surely spirits must go with him along his new way, and surely other men's bodies must die when the Chief's body is lifeless ; a burial solitary and without many dead to honour our Chief, this is fit only for a dog."

So say the men of Nias, who do not understand why the white man will not let them take heads from the defenceless.

In the southern part of the island there never was any headhunting, but, instead, skulls were bought from the peoples of the interior, weighed, I suppose, against leaf gold.

No tales of head-snatching had been carried to the Dutch Comptroller for several years till happened this tragedy of the Chief.

The old man was brought before us in manacles and hand-cuffs which he hardly needed. He was probably no more murderous in feeling than ourselves ; but usage hallows custom, and that was his custom. His son was with him.

The putting up of the camera terrified the older man ; perhaps he thought it was the first torture of the Dutch Government. Anyway, he fell on the ground half fainting. The outstretched palms shown in the photograph were his greeting of respect to us.

" Did you feel pity or scorn for the Chief when he half fainted ? " I asked Talbot, and he answered, surprised, " Why ? I felt neither ; I was intent on my work."

Judged by Mynheer van Vuuren, who summoned Chiefs of Nias to aid him in his jurisdiction, the Chief and his son were banished for twenty-five years to Sumatra. I am glad that the elder man escaped his punishment by dying a few months later in prison, but I suppose that his son is doing forced labour somewhere in Sumatra. The Netherlands' Government forbids capital punishment both in Holland and in the Dutch colonies.

Next came out three adulteresses, shy and prudish, with their cloths drawn high over them, and not, as is their custom, simply tied at the waist. Induced to be natural, they also were photographed; one of them appeared to be about sixty years of age. They were enduring three months' imprisonment, as were also their co-respondents, save one, who instead had paid a heavy fine.

In heathen Nias adultery was the worst crime, and both sinners were killed under the native law. Since there came the Dutch administration, the Nias code has been modified and unified, for it varied very much in different places. Now, adulterers, when brought to judgment by the Comptroller, who is aided by native rulers, have to pay six pounds, or suffer imprisonment. In some parts of Nias prostitutes also were killed, but in South Nias prostitution appears to be unknown. The price of women is very high, even one of low degree costing in pigs the value of from twenty to twenty-five pounds. Many Nias men must, therefore, live permanently virgin.

THE HEADHUNTERS.

Photograph by J. Talbot Clifton.

THE ADULTERESSES.

To face page 74.

CHAPTER XXI

BAWA SOWEA

" Travellers bring sugar-candy . . . as a present to their
friends,
Altho' I have no candy, yet have I words that are
sweeter."
SADI.

TWENTY hours of a swelling sea and then we reached
Telok Dalam, the port of Southern Nias, where is a
small military station, the soldiers of the garrison being
men of Java, under a Dutch Military Comptroller.
This officer greeted us on our arrival, and took us to
his bungalow to await our host, Herr R——, who was
coming from the Mission Station to fetch us. He
gave us native knives in wooden sheaths bound round
with metal, and we gleaned certain information about
South Nias. In the southern part of this island the
people have attained a far higher development than
have those of North or Central Nias. In the north
are straggling houses, and the natives are already
affected by contact with the white man ; in the centre
are unevolved Niasers, pig-hunters to-day, headhunters yesterday ; but in the south are large fortified
villages, chiefs, ancient customs, a profusion of gold
ornaments, and even a form of rude art, for the Southern
Niaser is a gifted sculptor. My spirits rose in excitement ; I longed to learn more of these people, so little
known.

Raffles visited Nias and even took possession of it for the British, but it probably is now much as it was then, save that the terrible Acheenese of Northern Sumatra, can no longer sweep down on Nias and carry off her sons as slaves.

Our host arrived in the evening, and we set out with two ponies between the three of us, animals we each in turn bestrode.

Against our wishes four or six Javanese soldiers were sent with us to form a guard lest the Niasers should not welcome our strange advent.

As we journeyed the ten or twelve miles which lay between the Mission Station and the harbour, Nias as fairyland became revealed.

First, in the moonlight, we saw the noble open country of Telok Dalam, undulating plains covered with coarse grasses. Beyond that we came to the lovely sands by the sea, whence huge rocks towered suddenly against the waves. Here slim coconut palms lifted their fine heights towards the blue immensity above them. Breathless with so much beauty we rode on till we came to Bawa Sowea, where is the Mission House, and at its gate Frau R——, in apron and print gown, welcomed us.

The dinner was of her own cooking and the beds were soft and warm—good comfort in the unexpectedly cold nights which here followed the burning days.

Even our matutinal bathing, prosaic function elsewhere, was here a rite worthy of Venus's self. Down a long flight of rough steps to the river-side I went, and there was a grotto, a place among the rocks, where fresh water ran. Swallows flew beneath the natural roof sheltering me, and fishes shared my delight in the water. Thus I bathed, but our host and hostess preferred their European tubs in their rooms. Indeed, the grotto seemed formed rather for pagan joys than for those serious people from the West. In the evening there were bats instead of swallows to watch me in the bathing place.

After breakfast, I went out with Herr R—— and sat by the sea till the sunlight on the waters dazzled us, then suddenly from the sands I saw steps which led steeply up the hill to a rude door in a rough stone wall, encircling something amid the palms.

I slowly climbed the hundred rugged steps that led to the door, pushed it open, and stood amazed in the first South Nias village I had seen.

It crowned the hill ; it was made strong with double walls ; it was paved with stone. On either side of that paving were houses, some twenty on each side. They were built, all of noble timber, like great sailing ships ; they stood on strong columns of wood. They were beautiful. In the space between the houses was a shrine holding the gods of the people, little figures of wood, images of departed parents. When a man dies, his likeness is carved in wood ; but strange to say, these images show the Niaser as a bearded man, though none I ever saw had hair upon his face. Whether this lack of beard is the result of custom or of nature, I never could discover.

The eldest son of a dying man breathes up the

departing spirit, and pressing his lips to his father's, he draws into himself the dying man's last sighs.

After the death of a man there is great clamour throughout the village. " Wake up ! Wake up ! " cry the mourners, not because they hope to summon back the soul if it be departed, but because they fear to take out into the jungle one who may not be dead. When sure that a man is dead, they take his body out to the jungle and leave it there, sheltered by a roof of thatched palm leaves raised up above the ground on stacks of wood.

To Lowalangi,[1] supreme God and Creator, the people of South Nias do not pray. He is too good to need appeasing, too great to be approached with human petitions, so it is to their parental deities. they turn ; but evil spirits are pacified with gifts.

In the heart, the centre of the village, were the seats of the Chief and of his sons, and on one of these stone thrones rested a youth whom I knew at once to be noble. His hair flowed down to his neck, whereas had he been a slave it would have been shorn. Pride and dejection were shown in his listless, unclothed body. Round his loins was draped a long pleated, many-coloured cloth. He wore a silver sword. In his black hair was a band of pure leaf gold, and a gold ornament encircled his neck. His slight proportions were perfect, but he was weak with fever.

The old forge was near the centre of the village, and here, in the past, were cast the swords and weapons, after which children are still named. No one now

---

[1] The name differs in various localities.

CROCODILE CARVED IN STONE.

THE SEATS OF THE CHIEFS.

To face page 78.

works at the bellows, and the anvil is cold. Fighting between the villages is forbidden by the Dutch, so weapons are not needed by the Chiefs. " The white men have come and have changed us into old women," they complain, and the young men hear them listlessly. Nothing is left in their lives save pigs and coconuts.

The wives of the Chief lament otherwise, saying, " Who is there to wait on us ?—we, who were nurtured in ease, have now no slaves."

The old Chief approached us and spoke sullenly to the Missionary, who was carrying his strongest walking stick, for this village was of all the most unfriendly. The enmity dated from Herr R——'s first visit, when the Chief, in return for the German's outstretched hand, offered him his foot ! The European promptly took it and swung the Chief backwards, which action has never been forgiven by the Nias ruler.

CHAPTER XXII

DELIGHT

" Ah, past the plunge of plummet,
    In seas I cannot sound,
My heart and soul and senses,
    World without end, are drowned."
                            A. E. HOUSMAN.

NIAS is as a song set to the measure of the sea's music, the great waters of which came much into our lives, for the delight of them crowned every day.   When the fearful glory of the sun had softened into purple and green and orange, we would go down to the sands and bathe in a pool where the sweet river water mixed with the salt.

The current here was rapid in places, and added to the excitement this gave me was the thrill of expectation caused by the nearness of crocodiles, for many were in the river, and one night I saw one pass me and swim towards the sea.

In a loose gown, almost nothing of a garment, I rested on the sands after playing in the sea pool. The waves came gently over me whilst the sunlight gave way to moonlight, and some fragment would flash into my mind, oftenest this, for so I felt :

.   .   .   .   .   " overbowed
By many benedictions—suns,
And moons and evening-stars at once.

> And so, you, looking and loving best,
> Conscious grew, your passion drew
> Cloud, sunset, moonrise, star-shine too,
> Down on you, near and yet more near,
> Till flesh must fade for heaven was here ! "

Yet the body too in such moments was a vehicle of delight, warmed by the tropic air, free to the breezes, washed by the tender waves. I felt often so happy that I would run for very joy upon the sands under the palms.

If men passed it was no matter, for they were children too. Unclothed themselves, they did not note my little clothing. Crowned with gold, they went with swinging steps on their homeward way. If a little fear did mingle with my pleasure in thus seeing them, it was fear they never gave me cause for.

Men had, on the first night, stood hidden among the palms, and suddenly I saw the glinting of their swords in the moonlight. Thinking they must be Niasers, I walked towards them, outwardly bold. I found but the Javanese soldiers practising war rites, because they thought the Niasers might attack me.

After that night the guardian Javanese were asked to keep to the Mission House and not to follow us, except when ordered to do so.

CHAPTER XXIII

CREATION OF MAN

"The Lord said to the angels, 'Verily I am creating a mortal from crackling clay of black mud wrought into shape ;

"And when I have fashioned it, and breathed into it of my spirit, then fall ye down before it, adoring.'

"And the angels adored all of them together, save Iblis, who refused to be among those who adored.

"He said, 'O Iblis ! what ails thee that thou art not amongst those who adore ?'

"Said he, 'I would not adore a mortal whom thou hast created from crackling clay of black mud wrought into form.'"

KORAN.

A GERMAN Missionary heard spoken in blank verse the following poem. Men of Nias, standing round the dead body of a Chief, thus spoke of the Creation of Man :

"The highest God arose,
There arose the highest God,
The great Lolo Zaho arose,
He went forth to bathe in the waters,
He went forth to bathe and to dive.
There alone by the spring like a mirror,[1]
There alone by the spring like a sheet of glass [1]
He took a lump of earth as big as an egg,

[1] Mirrors and glasses must have been known through the Chinese traders, who for centuries have visited Nias.

When he saw his shadow in the water,
When he saw his shadow in the depths,
He carried it under the meeting-house,
He carried it under the living-house,
His earth, his one handful,
His earth as big as an egg,
He formed it like the image of an ancestor,
He formed it like to a child.
His earth, his one handful,
His earth as big as an egg.
He fetched the scales of the measure,
He fetched the weights shaped like a hen,[1]
He laid it on the scales of the measure to weigh it.
He weighed the wind against the gold-dust,
He weighed the wind against the gold.
Then he laid himself on the lips,
He laid himself down to give out breath,
Then " it " spake like a child,
Then he spake like a man,
Spoke before the highest God,
Up there before Lolo Zaho.
The God gave to the man a name,
He gave a name when he was there.
Sihai de droben who has no descendants.
Sihai de droben who has no children.
And then rose up the highest God,
And then rose up the great Lolo Zaho.

Of the origin of the Nias people very little is known. It is thought they came from the west coast of Sumatra, and yet they have so much in common with the Dyaks that their origin may be the same as that of the people of Borneo. Many of them claim a super-mundane

---

[1] The people have weights of this shape.

83

origin and declare that their ancestors were left on various parts of the islands, plants and animals being sent to maintain them. The very word *Nias* means a man !

Their traditions are, of course, verbal ; they vary in every part of the isle. The poem I have quoted is southern.

Another legend runs that the people are born of the winds and air, that thirty winds met and gave life to two great trees set with fruit. From the fruits of one came the spirit of God, Lowalangi, from the other came that of Satan, Atocha. From the divine tree came also other shining spirits and gods, but from the vile tree came evil powers. Also the great gods Balin and Barasiluluo sprang from the tree of Lowalangi. Do these form with Him a Triune Power ? I think so.

Barasiluluo made a man and Balin added to him a soul, and they called him Tuha Nilolo. He had many children and they lived on planes above the earth, of which planes there are eight. At last, one forged the earth, but the foundations were not strong, and before the work was done the whole was destroyed in a mighty fall.

Then came a second celestial smith, and he made a better earth, for he laid his mother's rings under the globe and coconut leaves beside it. But Silewa, the mother of the earth's creator, changed her ring into a snake which still lies under the earth. When it turns, the earth shakes. Another saying about earthquakes is that the ancestors of men—of Niasers, that is—move uneasily in the earth, and the people when they feel the earthquake run out into the paths crying, "Great fathers, cause it to be not over terrible!"

From two great trees of the wind's creation came not only gods and spirits, beauty and harm, but also the moon, with her children the stars, likewise the sun, who devoured his children. Had he not done so the earth would have been over-hot.

CHAPTER XXIV

A NIAS BRIDE

"But, far from Him whom I adored,
My sleeve is wet with bitter rain—
Earthly and mortal I abide
From His dear Presence sundered wide."
(From the *Manyôshui.*)

HERE is a true story that I am going to tell you, that
you may feel the pulse of this remote people. I can
find no moral in it ; it was a tragedy for which none was
to blame. It was inevitable, this martyrdom in embryo.
Lions and tigers and jungles and gods cannot stand
out against the white man, who goes all over the world
seeking to gain wealth or to bestow salvation.

In this beautiful place the people are happy, as
among us only children are happy. Their belief in
fate is so strong that it saves their ever being much
troubled about anything. "He willed it so," they
say, when they see one dead, for they hold that the
body's destiny is described by the soul before the
body's birth. They brave death in ways that seem
foolish, go in boats full of flaws and leave fevers
undoctored, because they believe that all things are
pre-destined.

From a cobbler's house in Germany went a keen-
eyed, ambitious, believing man to Nias, in order to

persuade the people of Nias to think in the way that his Society considered the right way; he was a Missionary.

The Niasers had only seen white men coming to inhabit their country and rule their land. They had never even imagined that one would come who wanted nothing from them, but wished only to reign over their minds, and to sweep away their gods as the others had swept away their laws and customs. They wondered a good deal at his care for them. They liked him when he gave them medicines and ointments, though they never fully understood how wonderful it was that he should come hundreds of miles for their sakes, to live here, like a pine tree in a jungle, to do them good.

He set up a school where a native Christian from Sumatra taught the children to count, to speak Malay, and to find their places quickly in the Bible. He was human, therefore he enjoyed his new importance. It was pleasant to be in a community where he was the wonder-worker, the great man, the clever man ; where officials, when they passed his Mission Station, consulted him, where he knew no superior, either mental or social ; for as a cobbler in Germany he was hardly at that altitude.

Still, he often felt homesick and ill. He longed for his fatherland, and for all the things he had always known and liked; if suddenly his faith had gone he certainly would have found nothing in Nias to repay him for his sacrifices. He was not at all like a scientist or artist or philosopher, because nothing in Nias appealed to him except whatever was unhappy or wrong from his standpoint. He found no solace in nature ; he did not study nature. The people's modes of thought he considered merely foolish and quite uninteresting. A day came when he grew happier, for, after he had saved some money and improved his house, he wrote to Germany, to a girl interested in his Mission work whom he had long known. He asked her to come out and marry him. She did so. When writing home, she said how terrible it was that in Nias the meaning of " wife " was, " she who feeds the pigs."

She did almost all the cooking. Her paid servants, young converts, helped her hardly at all, nor could she trust them. She and her husband upset all the standards of the people whom they converted, and she could not but mark that they grew worse in spite of the Mission teaching.

When she heard the Nias children singing hymns to brass instruments, all dressed in German cotton pyjama-like suits, she smiled again, for she loved godliness with all her true heart, but she did not value beauty, and thought that men's bodies, which, before her coming, had been unclothed in all innocence and much grace, were unholy and evil things, though she also believed they were the images of God.

In fact she believed a great deal and thought very little, and she did unselfish things from the sunny morning to the mosquito-ridden night.

When the Grimms—let that be their name—had been for some time in the far-away island, they heard that a girl whom the Missionary had baptised was going to be married, that is, sold.

The women in Nias have a high price; they are valued against gold. They are proud of their worth, and secretly each one looked down on Frau Grimm, who had cost nothing.

"I should have plenty of wives if ours were as cheap as that," the Chief had said; but when he was told that not only had she not been paid for, but had actually brought money to her husband, the Chief's envy was boundless. At the same time, he pitied and despised the white woman for having had to pay to be married. Looking at her large and shapeless frame, he did not so much wonder.

The bride-to-be was a daughter of a Chief who had remained pagan, but who had not minded her being christened Salome, and his son Wilhelm.

One brilliant golden morning Salome, in great distress, visited Frau Grimm, and told her she was to be married to a young Chief in a far-off village, a heathen village. The Chief was a pagan.

"I shall forget Christ and you, and my singing and counting," she said, "for I cannot be Christian all alone so far away." Salome knew that the familiar carved figures of ancestors would soon reclaim her devotions and oust the new, invisible deity, but she feared the wrath of which she had been told so much. She knew that she had had her one chance, and that, whatever mercy might be found for those who had never heard of Christ, there could be none for her if she forgot Him.

At last, " Good-bye," she said, " but if I come late and knock, oh ! let me in ; yet I shall never see you again."

The Grimms promised her they would keep her and never allow her to be sold against her will. They let her return to her home, only because her father had promised her that she should be given time to reconcile herself to the marriage, and that if anyone else would bid as high for her as the Chief had done, she would be sold to him.

She had been taught by the Missionaries that the ways of her people were wrong, their nudity a blot on the earth, their gods loathsome, and she had believed it ; now came the bitter fruits of her adherence to the white man's faith.

That night Herr and Frau Grimm slept heavily. The latter dreamt of how to cook some tinned meat that had just reached her from Europe, the former of a new instrument that had arrived for their brass band. Salome beat in vain at the doors and called for her friends. She had discovered that the Chief was coming two days later to eat the nuptial feast and had escaped to the Grimms in desperation. Soon she was missed. Her brothers gagged her and dragged her back to her father's house. Already more than half her price, about fifty pounds' worth of gold leaf, had been paid by this distant Chief whom she had never seen. Hearing that, she yielded and made no more effort to save herself.

The day dawned with the usual brilliancy of all days in Nias, the village was astir to receive the bridegroom

THE SON OF A CHIEFTAIN.

To face page 90.

Chief. He came with slaves and his friends, with his warriors in helmets and in coats of crocodile skin. He had but a brilliant loincloth bound about his ivory-coloured body.

They danced, but Salome took therein no pleasure, as she had been taught by the Missionary that dancing was evil.

A pig roasted whole was eaten, and according to the marriage custom, Salome wept and screamed her fare-wells, but, unlike most Nias brides, she did not merely feign sorrow, but most bitterly she felt it. When she moaned the ancient words of her people: " Why should strangers part us, why should we be sundered ? " she spoke from her heart. She was dragged to the feast, and her bridegroom gave her golden presents, but she tore up the brittle leaf-gold things as she sat before the untasted food, scattering the precious frag-ments on the ground.

Lastly came the placing of Salome under a carved god, and a short blessing from the Chief, her father. Then, resisting, she was torn away and carried scream-ing from the village by one of the fighting men. In a week or ten days' time she would return with the bridegroom to her father's house, to give back the various ornaments and articles of clothing lent to her, and to bid a last farewell to her mother.

As a Chief's wife, she would be honoured in her new home. She would walk supported always by servitors, and would be the most cherished, or probably the only, wife of her husband. She would wear a crown of gold worked into flowers many inches high, and her husband's throne, carved in stone, would be in the centre of the village. But the big house rising from pillars of wood as though from roots, the polished central room with its armour and gods and old Chinese dishes—all were powerless to comfort Salome.

A boy was placed on Salome's knees as she entered her husband's house, a child of good omen, that she might bear sons and chiefs. The people called her "New Moon" and "Dawn of Day," whereas a despised bride and cheap, the bride of a poor man, they would have called "Hungry One."

Salome determined to die.

In vain were the caresses of her husband's family lavished upon her; she would not eat, she starved and pined away. Even the approaching visit to her mother did not sustain her; she had determined to die.

Seeing that all else was in vain, the young Chief summoned Salome's parents, though this was contrary to custom, but already it was too late, for Salome died of fever and starvation ten days after the wedding feast.

"It is a pity for the money's sake," said her husband, when he found her dead on her pallet, and that remained Salome's unwritten epitaph.

Photograph gift of a Missionary.

"THE BIG HOUSE RISING FROM ITS PILLARS OF WOOD."

To face page 92.

CHAPTER XXV

DAYS IN NIAS

" Remember that everywhere you will find some sort of faith and righteousness. See that you foster this and do not destroy." Asoka's " Charge to Missionaries."

Long, quiet days passed in Nias ; days of story-telling.

I heard Frau R—— telling to a Nias woman the story of Joseph and his brethren ; as she listened, she wept. Tolstoy also wept at this story. Tolstoy and the Nias woman ! Then, bit by bit, I gleaned the story of our hostess.

Herr R—— had first gone to Nias and she had followed. She knew him very little ; she had not seen him for years. She went out consumed with the zeal of his work, willing to devote herself to bringing Christ to Nias, very little caring for the man she was to marry, the instrument merely of her ideal. She was of the stuff that should form Missionaries—intense, eager, persuaded, narrow too. He was easy-going, larger minded, a little cynical perhaps. That she resented.

After years of life in Nias he made a few converts and started a school.

One day some half-converted men of Nias came sorrowfully to the Missionary. " How will our fathers be saved," they asked, "since they never heard of Christ, and without Him you say there is nothing but Hell?" The Lutheran answered; "Your fathers will perhaps find pity, and a chance of Heaven may be offered to them. Christ once preached to souls in Hell; He could do so again. The urgent matter is that, for you, this message of mine is your sole hope. If you do not seize the truth you will be bound, and cast into Hell by an angel of God."

The people, upon that, became Christian. The school house was used as a church on Sundays, and the work prospered. (This happened in the North of Nias.)

Then for a short time the Missionary left his home and his wife; he had been sent on a visit to a distant station, whither a friend of his had just gone. One night a storm raged and lightning struck the school house, which was burnt completely down. When the German returned there was nothing left but the house he had lived in.

The converts said, "If the work was pleasing to God, why did His lightning destroy it?" and they ceased to believe. Because the now broken-hearted German woman had seen the finger of God in every plank of the Mission Church, she too felt her faith scorched.

They left that part of Nias and came here, where they had some young scholars but no converts.

Our hostess, every morning, sat in the drawing-room and watched her Nias boy dusting the faded photograph of the Königin Louise coming downstairs.

Every day, except on Sundays, the picture was cleaned and replaced on a small table heaped with pathetic remembrances of Germany. Afterwards the boy, in dreary routine, passed a linen duster over the poker-work texts nailed to the wall and across the painted looking-glass.

When the dusting was done she would go to the kitchen to cook the mid-day meal. " I work less hard here than I should in Germany," she said, when I offered to help her.

One day our noon-time feast was varied by the appearance of meat. This luxury we expected only at the end of the week, for every Saturday a soldier from Telok Dalam brought some from the small harbour garrison as a gift to the Mission House. On other days we ate eggs, rice, vegetables and preserved fruits from Germany. This meat had a curious taste, as though it should have gone bad but had been prevented from doing so by some law stronger than that of natural decay.

" May I ask if this meat is tinncd or fresh ? " queried the Explorer. Frau R—— replied : " I cannot say that it is either." Turning to her husband, she asked, " Do you remember the cow we had at Gunung Sitoli five years ago ? " " I remember it well," he mused. " When we left I had it killed, and we put some meat in our sterilizer. It has been there ever since," she continued happily, and whilst we paused with drooping forks above our fare, our host turned on us his good Teuton smile and said, " Ah ! It is fine—our sterilizer. So long we have kept this beef; but now we are able to set it before you, our honoured guests."

Truly even the laws of Nature prove impotent faced by the genius of the true *hausfrau* !

After our mid-day meal we would rest till, at half-past three, delicious cake and coffee were set before us. Afterwards we visited hamlets, or went down to the sea to bathe, until the evening meal was served.

CHAPTER XXVI

THE VILLAGE OF A CHIEF

"Whereas in myself I mean to be kindly I must often
be taken as rude. How can I not be strange to one who
has never wandered in the Sun?"

PARACELSUS.

On the last day in South Nias we visited Kanôlôô, the
Chief of the village of Hiliganowô.

"Wer seine Frau schätzt
Lässt sie zu Hause!"

hummed Herr R——, when I asked if Frau R——
would not come with us.

Near the village were sweet water baths, shut in by
high walls. The women's bathing place lay apart from
the men's and was guarded by inviolate law, for death
was deemed the proper punishment to him who should
intrude on women bathing.[1] Calling out loudly a
warning of our approach, our host led me to this
sanctuary. I went in among the women who were
drawing water and cooling themselves in the running
stream that passed through their bathing place. The
walls guarding it and the stones paving it were over-
grown with ferns, its roof was the firmament.

By the sea were low stone seats, whereon sat

---

[1] A heavy fine is now imposed by the Chiefs.

young Nias men looking out lazily over the waters. Only Gauguin could paint them with their strange charm.

From the foot of the hills started a long flight of rude steps leading steeply to the double walls and the gates of the village. A path ran up a further part of the hill under the palms, but we chose the six hundred steps, for near them we could see rough memorials of the dead, wooden shrines hung with rags, and dishes, and odd treasures, left there to symbolise the thoughts of the living for the dead.

Up the six hundred steps through the gates, on to the flagged street, past the thatched shrine of the ancestor-gods, into the house of Kanôlôô, we went.

Into the great central room of the Chief's house we climbed, going up a ladder which led from under the building into this wide upper hall, which was most beautiful. The walls were of polished wood hung about with tusks of boars and the horns of deer, of which the antlers had but six tines at most. Big Chinese plates were suspended from the raftered ceiling, some being enclosed in wicker baskets. Others hung revealed, their colours blending with the blue and old rose painted bowls which also came from China. These bowls were used for the washing of the hands of guests after food.

There were no windows, but a kind of wide lattice ran round one side of the hall. Below the lattice was the large curved wooden seat of the Chief and of his sons, the seat being raised above the floor by long, shallow steps.

THE BOYS OF NIAS.

THE GODS OF NIAS.

Photograph gift of a Missionary.

To face page 98.

The fireplace was very handsome. It stood on carved legs of wood, raised from the ground, and its sides were supported by wooden pillars. It came far out into the room; in its centre stood a brazier wherein was the fire. The tall image of a god was near. Beyond stood the peeping women of the house, watching us with dark eyes, their small heads shaved closely, save where, in the centre of the head, a knot of hair was allowed to grow.

Kanôlôô had his warriors. He offered to show us their method of war dance and of fighting. Then he left us to clothe himself in his warrior dress.

When we had arrived in the morning he had been wearing a coloured jacket of stiff material and a pleated loin cloth; round the thick dark hair that fell on to his neck he had wound a coloured cloth.

When he reappeared in his martial dress it seemed we lived on another star or in another age. He shone with gold. A band of the yellow metal crowned his head, and from it rose flowers of gold, rudely formed, but pleasing. Heavy circles of gold were on his wrists, on his neck were ornaments of leaf gold. His jacket was of thick woven stuff, striped red, blue, white and yellow, and below it he wore balls of coloured wools to make the garment stand well out. A brilliant loin cloth fell below this jacket. Most remarkable of all was his sword sheathed in gold, with a handle shaped like a monkey's head with eyes of rubies, and enriched with tigers' teeth. He was amazing and splendid, and as dignified as in his simple clothing, but not more so. He then called on his men, and we pressed against the open squares in the room of our reception, to see them gathering below.

Like a play from Shakespeare, they prefaced their dancing with a speech. They assured us that they meant no harm, that all would end in peace, and then the war dance began.

The warriors came towards each other from either end of the village, advancing by two steps and retiring by one with each third movement. Slow progress, you may imagine! The men wore metal helmet caps, protecting only their heads, but not their faces. Their projecting jackets, which on working days are of roughest coconut fibre, had now been replaced by coats of crocodile skin. They carried spears, and cried out, "Ha, ha!" and sang shrilly as they advanced, their wooden shields before them. When the opposing bodies met at last, they rushed together, stamping and spearing and clashing their shields.

When all was over Kanôlôô gave us some helmets and jackets, and we gave him silk in exchange, with which he would pay the Chinese for plates, or tiger teeth, or a little alcohol, if he dared to break Dutch laws. The Niasers of the South never drink to excess as do the Northerners, who make their own strong spirit from the fruit of a certain palm.

I felt sad at leaving the island, and through our German host I told the Chief of my regrets. "Your heart is hairy," was his unexpected answer; and I learned that, when the heart is hairy, it is in pain.

Among the people of Nias the heart is the centre of thought, understanding and feeling. It 'hurts' when a man is jealous, it 'grows big' when he loves, and 'broad' when he is patient and foreseeing. When he is insulted it is shaken, and it censures him in his hours of remorse, but when he is utterly discomforted or surprised it 'dies' within him. Finally, when his body is dead and cradled in his coffin among the trees, the 'Mōkōmōkō' rises up and leaves the body in the jungle, and goes on its mysterious way. The mōkōmōkō is the soul of the heart, the part that lives when the man is dead, whilst his spirit enters into his son. For 'flesh' the people of Nias have no word in their language.

Kanôlôô and most of his men are now gathered to their ancestors, for a great sickness smote the village soon after we left Nias, but when I think of Hiliganowô without him, the whole world seems to have lost a grace.

CHAPTER XXVII

NAKO

"I do not doubt that wrecks at sea, no matter what the horrors of them—no matter whose wife, child, husband, father, lover, has gone down, are provided for to the minutest point."

WALT WHITMAN.

THE first of April dawned, and was the day when we had to leave Nias, and sail for the island of Nako.

After a farewell said in regret and gratitude to our hostess, we rode to Telok Dalam with Herr R——— and embarked for Nako where, for an hour or two, a steamer called every month.

All day we sailed on seas intensely blue, made fragrant by lovely islands, like bunches of flowers thrown on the waters.

When in the evening we reached Nako, Herr Hoffmann, German evangelist to the isles, met us in a rowing boat, for he had had previous news of our coming. In the bay, under the little boats, the sea was turquoise and bright green, whilst the coconut palms threw shades that seemed not shadows but rather rainbows on the waters.

Sad seas and bitter, for, in spite of their glory of colour and breeze-borne fragrance, they are a canopy to other things as terrible and lovely as themselves. All the swords, shields, spears and armoury, all the symbols of savage manhood, the proudly held ancestral war tools, lie in the sea. The people had to bring them here in boats and lower them into the depths, losing them for ever, because in these ten islands of Nako, and more especially in the central one, the fighting and killing were so unending that the Dutch commanded that all weapons should be thrown into the sea. The men of Nako have forged no others.

Also, in accordance with their own law in the past, all the lovers of the islands were drowned in these smiling seas ; for woman here is bought, and she must not be stolen, nor can she bestow herself on any man unless he can pay her price in leaf gold or in swine.

So, in the shifting sands, lie those who, without weighing their desires against the sum of purchase, loved with the forbidden love. They were drowned together when the sin was known to the pitiless men of Nako. Lovers and swords are in the sea, whilst their gods are ashes thrown to the listless winds. I speak with certain knowledge only of those ancestral images which were adored on the isle that we knew. All of them were burnt on one day by the Lutheran Missionary.

He had four hundred Christians under him now, and there are some seventy Mahommedans among the islanders.

The lesser people of Nako originated from North Nias and number about two thousand five hundred souls, but the Chiefs, who are many, are thought to have come long ago from Bengal.

Next day we saw these Chiefs, when they came to entertain us, and their women with them. These rulers have intermarried for generations, but the race seemed a fine one, clearer skinned and more intelligent than the lower people.

The men danced boisterously and clownishly to amuse us, but the movements of the dancing women were slow and tense. Five of them had high crowns of gold, moulded into patterned flowers and leaves. Thirty of them had beautiful plain bands in their hair, and among them was Edelstein.

We noticed her at once, for she alone was beautiful. Pale ivory coloured and gracious, a very princess, she was dressed in golden silk, she had a girdle of gold and silver and a golden band in her hair. She was the daughter of a Chief and the wife of a Chief. The Missionary had baptised her and called her Edelstein— "precious stone." His eyes shone with gladness when we admired her. We beckoned her, and I felt that if we had had a mutual tongue she and I might have loved each other. She was apart from the rest, not only by her youth and beauty, but by a graciousness in her movements and by the wide intelligence of her eyes. Her husband, too, was fine to see. She had cost fine gold. I could imagine her, alone of all the eastern Christians I have seen, finding the core of her new creed and having joy of it.

These islanders are not fond of the Netherlands' rule, and when a Dutch official came to visit Nako they refused to appear in festal dress or to dance. Herr Hoffmann told me how he had expelled the fear of evil spirits and filled the people's minds instead with the fear of the invisible microbe of disease, against which his filter stood—a new form of charm.

A little while before we came to Nako, a young German and his wife had been sent there to do the work of Herr Hoffmann, who for a short time went to Europe. One stormy night the young man was summoned to another island. He noticed that the boat was hardly watertight, but to the boatmen that seemed nothing, for " what will happen, will happen." He started away and was drowned. Those who survived him ran to the Mission House to tell his wife what had happened. She had to find her written list of words and trace out one by one the awful few that bore her sentence of sorrow. Then the people left her, for even faith in fate could not detain them beneath a roof so struck by calamity. No one would serve or help the unhappy woman ; she remained alone until she was taken away from Nako by the authorities in Nias.

CHAPTER XXVIII

MENTAWI

" Like a taper one must melt in pursuit of learning."
SADI.

FROM Nako we returned to Nias and reached it adventurously riding the surf in a canoe. We crossed Nias from East to West, riding and walking and spending the nights in fortified military encampments. Thence we returned to Padang.

A fateful map spurred Talbot's desires towards the group of Mentawi Islands.

The captain of the steamer, which once a month takes mails to the Military Comptroller, said, " You should not go; no traveller ever lands there, for the islands are under martial law. I have only taken there the Dutch Military Comptroller, Javanese soldiers, and Javanese convicts to cut down the jungle, and three German Missionaries, of whom one died of blackwater fever, another was murdered by the men of Mentawi, and the third has not been there long. Lawless savages might kill you ! You will be covered with sores ! " Thus he admonished us.

We said : " Take us with you ! We shall at least see if we are allowed to land at Siberoot. Our letter from the Governor of the West Coast of Sumatra may enable us to do so."

He took us. When we reached Siberoot we were allowed to land.

We had brought no provisions with us, so the captain of our ship sold us some eggs and bacon, and kindly gave us bread and meat. With a final warning, he sailed away.

At Siberoot, we learned that the *Ceram*, a small military ship, was lying in the harbour. Next day she was to sail for North Pageh, carrying the Eurasian Military Comptroller to that island, as also Dr. Van der Kloet, who was to inspect medically a small garrison between Siberoot and North Pageh, also to visit the Military Station at North Pageh.

Captain Berlyn, a most charming man, was in command of the *Ceram*.

On the *Ceram* with us was the Military Comptroller and his enormous white wife, who, clothed in native garments, sang all through the day teasing music-hall melodies, only breaking off to talk to the little Javanese serving girl, who sat on the deck at her mistress's naked feet. I think the lady had been on the stage, but we could not converse much as she spoke only Dutch. She never came to meals with her husband, of whom later we saw a good deal.

After a long day of the sea and of shrill singing, we reached the island of Sipora in the evening, and landed the doctor who inspected the handful of soldiers in the barracks.

Talbot and I walked down a track in the jungle. He suddenly felt ill, sick in fact, and asked me to go on alone for a little way. Presently I had a sensation of someone behind me, and turning round I found myself looking into the dark eyes of a Mentawi savage.

He carried a knife wherewith to cut the roots or herbs he needed, and he was naked except for a loin cloth. He was tattooed with blue fantastic lines that ran from his body up over his face, and in his long hair he wore flowers and black strings, with here and there some beads tied round his head. Up and down my spine I felt a curious irritation, because I had seen the knife in his hand.

I walked on some way muttering to myself the historical "tu trembles carcasse," and then sat down by the wayside to let the Mentawian pass. As he did so we exchanged a frank stare and a faltering smile. Soon afterwards Talbot joined me.

That night we sailed for North Pageh.

On board were three Javanese destined to relieve the keepers of a lighthouse for which the *Ceram* was bound, and on the morrow we landed on a coral island, where a few coconut palms raised brave columns above the flaring shingle; on this beach stood the beacon.

On the shingle were large round holes caused by turtles coming up from the sea by night and laying in these simple nests their many eggs. The eggs are round and look like ping-pong balls; the shell is so soft that it becomes indented by the lightest touch.

When, later in the day, I ate one of the eggs, I found it gritty, and it tasted of fish.

Large baskets of these eggs are collected by the lighthouse men and sold to Chinese traders, who pay a high price for them and take them away in sailing boats.

That day we crossed the Straits of Sipora and reached our destination on the island of North Pageh.

CHAPTER XXIX

NORTH PAGEH

"I will wander all the world over and return to the
home of my fathers to muse on the strange and beautiful
things I have seen."

PIERRE LOTI.

LADEN with gift of bread, meat and vegetables, we took
our leave of Captain Berlyn and landed next day on
North Pageh to take up our habitation in the Rest House.
This had been built for a doctor who once lived there
awhile when the Dutch first took possession of the
Mentawi group. Captain Berlyn promised to be back
in a few days' time.

As a rampart to Sumatra and for general strategical
purposes Mentawi is thought to be of value to the
Netherlands, but it is too unhealthy and too undeveloped
to be of any other value.

Just before we landed Abraham had fallen ill with
malarial fever, so we wrapped him up in our coats and
gave him quinine and tinned fruits. He shivered and
burned in varying cycles of misery, and seemed as
though he had no sinews left wherewith to face the
headache and the thirst that tormented him. The
Military Comptroller, Captain van Geer, allowed us the
use of one of the Javanese convicts, for in Pageh there

are, besides the Javanese soldiers, a few long term men from Java who cut roads through the jungle and work for the little garrison.

Helped by this convict, I unpacked our cooking utensils. I spoke to the convict in what little Malay I could summon, and the following conversation between Talbot and myself was the result. He was on the verandah brushing away some ants, or perhaps trying to rid the air of mosquitoes by smoking, when I called out, " Talbot, we have a convict servant."

" Let's hope he's not a thief."

I, joyfully, "Oh! No, it's all right; he's killed somebody."

Talbot: " Splendid ! "

And thus began our housekeeping in Mentawi.

I later knew that our servant had killed a friend of his upon his refusing to repay a debt of one shilling, and, therefore, I right promptly paid this servant the pittance that we were allowed to give him. Indeed, I generally gave it to him in advance.

He was a melancholy youth, and I pitied him. Secretly we gave him tobacco and other small gifts not generally allowed to convicts.

He liked serving us, but laboured half-heartedly. Who, living in Mentawi as a convict, could keep a whole heart ? When he wearied of us, he ran to the prison to rest !

When Abraham recovered from the fever, he used to sing to the murderer long passages from the Koran, in a curious monotone, which recital would last far into the night. Strange nights ! Shall I ever forget them ?

"THE DEAR JAMBOSA"

Eugenia Jambos.

To face page 110.

After the heat, and hunger, and long hours of the day, of which I shall tell anon, there came often suddenly from across the Straits of Sikahap, from the island of South Pageh, first a cooling breeze, full of scent, then a great noise and a roaring of waters, as across the bay rushed the wind and the rain, up towards us. On the trees and the house the rain beat furiously. The jambosa in the garden, the dear jambosa which I had seen flowering in Sumatra and fruiting in Nias, shivered in the storm's strength, and dropped its fruits into the sodden earth.

Then the rain stopped abruptly, thunder filled the vaults of heaven, and forked lightning shot out. All the hills were visible in the lightning, and so were the trees. I could see them, tall and white stemmed, from my camp bed in the verandah. The storms were wilder and more primeval here than in any other land. When they passed away in the morning we would be awakened by crying and laughing, by a wild exultation, and a strange pæan rising up to the sun, to the eye of the day.

In the jungle round about us a thousand apes or more were greeting the dawn.

CHAPTER XXX

A WALK

"In this playhouse of infinite forms I have had my play."
                                                    R. TAGORE.

"Our old moon put her horns away, and the dark nights
        were three ;
    There danced a girt moon through the clouds, pallid as
        ivory,
    At break of day went Jupiter, patrolling down the sky,
    Just as a lonely watchman with a lantern passing by."
                                                    TBN AL MOTAZZ.

A MORNING dawned when we set out for Simon Tobi, the oldest and biggest village in North Pageh.

It was some fourteen miles from the barracks, and Lieutenant Van Geer, the Military Comptroller, wished to visit it, so he allowed us to join him with his escort of some twenty Javanese soldiers and a Dutch sergeant who could speak the Mentawi language.

The Lieutenant never went to any of the villages without a large military escort, and he was very anxious that we should always go protected in a like manner, but afterwards at times we evaded the guard and went with Herr Bürger, the German Missionary, who knew the people. I felt safer when unaccompanied by soldiers, for the natives might well have cause for anger and revenge at seeing us approach their hamlets with armed men.

MAN AND WOMAN OF MENTAWI.

To face page 112.

The path we followed through the jungle was just broad enough for two to walk abreast, and it ran four days' journey into the island.

High trees loomed above this tract, and wild banana palms overshadowed it, whilst huge rattan palms threw their thorny lassos about the deep thickets.

Every twenty minutes the sergeant called a halt, and for ten minutes the booted and over-clothed Javanese soldiers rested, but the Explorer fretted at the delay, for the hours moved on to the burning noon. Probably never had the soldiers marched so fast, for Talbot now set the pace. When the sergeant wanted to shoot at a bird he would call " Halt "; at other times he talked to his lieutenant who, in broken English and French, translated his questions to me.

Lieutenant van Geer, translating from the sergeant, an ex-waiter, spoke to me thus : " My sergeant would wish to know if you are very poor, as otherwise why should you come to Mentawi and always wear the same hat ? "

I explained that beyond suffering from the chronic poverty of the supposedly rich it was not extreme pauperism that had brought us to Mentawi, and that our method of travelling demanded the least possible luggage.

" I hate the Dutch; I should like to be a British officer," next said Lieutenant van Geer, kicking a dog which had neared us from the hamlet. He also confided : " I hope I shall never have to fight; I cannot bear the sight of blood. I trust that, if ever I am wounded, it may be in my back, where I shall be unable to see the wound."

I was shocked at his ingratitude, as the Dutch give a status to the Eurasian which certainly is not enjoyed by Eurasians in British Dominions.

At the next pause he examined my gold watch bracelet, which partly counteracted the bad effect of the only hat.

CHAPTER XXXI

SIMON TOBI

"There are savages who seem to civilized men to have
no moral sense; but those who know them best discover
that their lives are governed by the strictest rules of
conduct, that they are more conventional than any early
Victorian old maid."

SIMON TOBI lay embowered in flowers; hibiscus
flamed about it, whilst cannas and orchids were
massed near a thick hedge of bamboos. The whole
village was railed in with bamboos.

"How strange for savages to have brought all these
from the jungle and to have planted them here," said
Talbot. Then we were given the reason for so much
beauty.

The wealth of flowers, the brilliant crotons, the
bushes were for the dead.

The lives of these people are beset with fear of their
departed friends, who when dead become devils and
torment them.

We walked down one of the long, clean paths, past
the great dwelling houses, with their thatches coming
down almost to the ground. In the river we saw two
women with nurslings at their breasts. They sat all
day in the river, clothed in thick dresses of leaves and

large leaf-plaited hats. Over the water the devils could not reach them and molest their infants, therefore they sought safety in the shallows of the stream.

We were hot, tired and thirsty. The Mentawei people saw our state; they cut branches from the palms for us to sit on and gave us water from the coconuts. They had never seen a white woman before, and they all stood near us and looked and girded at us. They laughed because I am so tall, and they are only about five feet high.

They did not insist on solving their doubt as to whether I was white all over, though for a few tense minutes it seemed as though they would forcibly unclothe me. I had some biscuits which I gave them, and they let us photograph them.

The natives of Simon Tobi would not let us enter their houses, and that day we saw only the outside of their daily lives. The people were in mourning for one dead, and wore no beads or flowers, nor would they dance.

When we were refreshed we walked through the village with the Comptroller, who brought a Javanese soldier to interpret into Malay the speech of the men of Mentawi. Thus we learned a little of the ways of the inhabitants.

We came upon the Place of Offerings—a long building surrounded with a wild profusion of flowers. The people prevented us from entering the house, and it was only later that I learned how the sacrifices are offered.

At the far end of the building the young men sleep,

Photograph by J. Talbot Clifton.

"THEY LET US PHOTOGRAPH THEM."

To face page 116.

but in the entrance hall, over which the great rafter hangs, there is in the floor a hole, into which falls the blood of any stag that is brought in from the jungle.

The stag is hung head downwards over the hole, and the priest calls out loudly again and again to the soul of the deer which is still in the jungle. When the soul returns to the body the meat is full of strength, and then the people are given their portions, which they eat, still calling on the soul. The children have a special share to strengthen their youth.

Of the priests I could discover but little. It would seem they have a certain power and magic—probably devilish rather than good.

One of the strangest houses was the house of a nymphomaniac—" everybody's fish " they called her, and she lived alone, scorned. I was told that such a house exists in every village of the island.

A woman of Mentawi is usually married after having had one child or more, though it is not always the child's father who marries her. There is no marriage ceremony, but it seems to be a custom that finally the woman remains with a certain man. She is faithful to him, and he adopts her children. A woman may kill her child if she cannot feed it from the breast. The people of Mentawi have no chiefs, no laws and no religion, but only superstitions. Besides suffering from the fear of devils, these people labour under a dreadful form of socialism.

A man will be sitting quietly with his companions, looking at the communal fields beyond the village or watching the pigs. If such a man has succeeded more than another of his village, if his palms have borne many nuts, or if his pigs have thriven exceedingly, he will suddenly be seized from behind and be bound and cast into a canoe, and so taken past the river, or across the sea, in grim haste to the burying-place in the jungle. He will be hung upon a tree till his soul, escaping, becomes one of that dread host which must be pacified by means of flowering shrubs and by blossoming flowers.

Before leaving the village, we saw, in front of one of the large *oemoer*—or dwelling-houses, houses which hold over a hundred people—a little girl with her mother and sisters. Beneath her amber skin she was fearfully pale, for she had been stung on her leg by a snake. Healing herbs had been applied to the wound, but it was now gangrenous and horrible to see. Thus she had been for days and would be till she died, except that each day would add to her pain. I gave the child all the rest of my biscuits, which, generous as are most savages, she divided amongst her sisters. Through the interpreter, I begged her mother to let me take the child back to the Mission House. I explained that by cutting off her leg her life might be saved.

They did take her to the Mission House, and her father left her there, but after a little while he returned, saying : " Better she should die if she cannot walk," and gently lifting her up took her back to Simon Tobi to die of the poison.

At length it was time for us to return, and the soldiers were ordered to march back, whilst we decided

to go by canoe.   Oh, the tedium of that journey !
In spite of my amusement at the Comptroller continually asking Talbot if he were afraid of these native
boats and the rage of my husband at the question, in
spite of the beauty of the natives standing at either end
of the dug-out, peacefully speeding us on by their
rhythmic steering fore and aft with long oars, the way
seemed very long.   We had to sit crouching on our
thighs on a few inches of hard wood, instead of a seat.
At last I could bear it no longer—I moved.   The dug-
out turned on the outrigger, the savages cried aloud,
and by good fortune only did the little vessel right
herself, though water had run over her sides and half-
filled her.

A moment later a large shark passed us, and there-
after I sat motionless for another long hour, when at
last we arrived at the Rest House that we now called
" home."

CHAPTER XXXII

THE LAST OF MENTAWI

"From a corner ran out Fever, long and slender, with ugly yellow face and dry bony hands, lay down beside him, embraced him, kissed his face and smiled."

The Herald of the Beast, by SOLOGUB.

THE Captain of the *Ceram* had promised that he would return after a few days, but a month went by, during which we vainly scanned the horizon for a trace of smoke. In desperation, we thought out a wild plan, and had we been abandoned much longer, we should have attempted to sail away.

The reasons for our discontent were several, of which the most vital was the lack of food. To prove how little food we had, be it known that one day, having found an egg, we fried it and solemnly divided it. Another trial was that we were covered from head to foot with sores; something in the climate caused our skin to become so tender that the rubbing even of a sleeve or of a shoe lace was sufficient to raise a blister.

Night brought no solace, for the sand flies penetrated through our mosquito nets and tortured us. Abraham was bidden to light fires that the smoke might keep them away, but he usually now wore bound

round his forehead a white handkerchief, which indi-
cated headache or lack of zeal. " A flag of truce,"
Talbot called it. Abraham was daily becoming more
and more insolent.

Once we tried to get food by joining the natives
when they hunted with arrows for deer on the Isle of
South Pageh, and once we went out fishing. Escaping
the vigilance of the soldiers, we went alone with some
Mentawi men. Whilst fishing, we saw great sun-
whales basking near the surface; but I was nearly distracted by the heat, the fearful glare, the heavy roll,
the narrow boat. I have never suffered so much from
the sun before or since.

On the day of our hunting in South Pageh we nearly
lost our lives.

We were returning in a canoe, when suddenly the
wind rose with a scream; the boatmen seized a banana
leaf, which they had brought to wrap their food in, and
one man held this upright to form a sail. With wild
gestures they made us understand that they needed
Talbot's coat as well. Death grinned in wind and
waves. The natives, whose despair was now visible,
nevertheless continued to hold up the makeshift sails,
until a furious gust of wind tore them from their
trembling hands. The Strait of Sikahap lay between
us and North Pageh, but should we make North Pageh
or Eternity? So I wondered, and then we were somehow blown on to the shore and safety.

The jungle was so dense and the earth so slippery
that it was too much of an effort often to walk abroad.
One track led to the Mission House, the other to

the barracks, where lived the Eurasian Comptroller, Lieutenant van Geer, and the Javanese soldiers. These soldiers received war pay, because it was considered that life in Mentawi was as hard as life on a campaign.

Fatima, as I called the obese and limping wife of the Comptroller, had never left her verandah during the entire month that she and we had been on the island. She was afraid even to leave the house; she had not yet seen an aboriginal. She was wonderfully contented, however. All day she sang the same little air. Her dog barked, and her Javanese maid talked to her, and they prepared salads from plants which a former Comptroller had planted. She pleaded with me to visit her father's grave in Holland. Save for this and for her little music-hall ditty, I should never have associated her with Europe. Certainly she had more Eastern than European blood.

I was solaced by the black herons with red beaks that fished in the blue waters, and the green birds with bright red circles round their eyes and a russet glow on their necks that flew about among the clerodendrons. I had a friend in the sea; "Ami," I called him. Later I found a picture of another such as he, whereby I learned that he was a fire-fish. The fish were fairy-like in their colouring; I never tired of watching them; as beautiful as flowers or jewels, the sea was a dream of colour. "No wonder pearls come from such waters," said Talbot. Blue was the colour of Mentawi; blue was the sea, blue fish swam therein; below, the coral reefs shone blue, and even the droppings of the birds were blue.

After more than thirty days had passed, suddenly we saw smoke and joyfully acclaimed the *Ceram*. Shortly afterwards she steamed in, and Captain Berlyn explained that she had had to have some repairs done, hence the delay in returning. He tarnished a little my joy in departing by refusing to take Abraham. I pleaded and begged in vain ; he would not help a rude native. The Comptroller had complained of Abraham. He promised to take him away the next time the *Ceram* called. I hope he did so, for it seemed heartless to leave our beautifully clothed little rebel on the island.

The heat, the insects, the hunger, our sores and the tedium of the life had indeed made us wish to leave North Pageh. We sailed on a swelling sea, reached Padang, thence took steamer to Batavia, from whence we hoped to travel to the Moluccas, of which we had heard alluring tales. Sailing, we passed by jungles wherein tigers lurked, and skirted the islands of Engano, which seemed to me more tragic than any others I had heard of. The dwellers there were Christian and very wealthy, for they had coconut plantations and had traded over a long period with the Chinese. They possessed pianos, gramophones and heavy velvet-covered furniture ; but a strange doom lay upon them, for they were unable to reproduce their race. No children gladdened their homes ; they saw their people dying out. A party of them once went to Java and stole some babies, but these were taken from them by the Dutch authorities, and they returned home child-less to face their barren wives and long, aimless lives from which would spring no young existences, until at last a two-fold death should wipe them from the earth.

When we reached Batavia I felt ill, and at Djokja-karta, wherefrom we meant to see the Boro Budur, I had a temperature of 104°. I lay down and tried to will away the fever. A superb exaltation resulted from this dramatic effort. Shivering and sickness followed, with all the train of fever symptoms.

The next day I was still fever stricken and very ill, so we determined to push on to the hills and leave unvisited the ancient glories of Java. After about twenty hours' journey we arrived at Tosari. There the doctor announced that I had blackwater fever.

END OF BOOK I

BOOK II

Oh ! can you bear
To let the beauty of the earth
Lie everywhere
Spread out beyond you ?   You not seeing it.

But do you know
Of perfumed seas, of tropic trees
Where orchids grow ?
Or know the sun can burn as fierce as love ?

Reading, maybe,
Some man, cooped in the Western world
Will feel, through me,
A craving for the East.   That man's my friend.

I used to give
Glory to God for places far away.
        Because I knew
        That in them grew
        Orchids and aloes.
Now I upraise my hands in praise
For all the beauty in my days
Spread from the Andes far as Halmaheira.

                                    VIOLET CLIFTON.

CHAPTER I

CELEBES

" But all the tune that he could play
Was : 'Over the hills and far away ! ' "
Nursery Rhyme.

MEA CULPA ! Mea culpa ! I had spoiled the last
journey. We had letters that would have helped us
in the Bismarck Archipelago, and we should have seen
these islands instead of waiting and wasting at Tosari
for me to get well, which I could not do. It took a
year of Lancastrian and Hebridean winds to blow the
fever out of me.

In 1921 Celebes called to Talbot. I never knew
quite how or why it did so. The first sign that I was
given was the *Encyclopaedia* open on the library table.

Perhaps it was the scarcity of roads in Celebes that
was the lure, or, far more probably, it was the wealth
of the island in birds and beasts that enthralled Talbot.
Reason enough for the open book and the telegram
ordering khaki clothes, was the anticipation of seeing
creatures not existing elsewhere. Hawks attract the
Explorer, and there are six species of hawks peculiar
to Celebes, whilst a seventh is found only in Celebes
and in the Island of Bangaya, whilst seven of the ten
kinds of parrot that decorate the jungles are never seen
save in that oddly shaped island.

The charming woodpecker family has but three branches in Celebes. These three are found only there.

The rose-chafers number thirty, nineteen of them live only in Celebes.

Five singular cuckoos inhabit the island, and the two varieties of hornbill differ slightly from those of other countries. Of starling parentage, there are six offshoots the like of which is not found the world over.

Here and there a bird bearing no resemblance to any Asiatic or Australian fowl reminds the naturalist of an African species, and there is a legend, semi-scientific, that when the world was very young Celebes[1] and Africa were joined together.

Eighteen kinds of pigeon coo and shimmer in Celebes; of them as many as eleven are known only in that Wonderland.

The tale grows in wonder. Out of fourteen terrestrial mammals that have their being in Celebes eleven of the number live almost solely there.

The most important of these are the baboon-like monkeys (Cynopithecus nigrescens)[2] and the Anoa depressicornis, or Sapi-utan, the creature that links up the ox and the antelope, and Africa with Celebes.

Strange as any is the Babirusa,[3] or hog-deer, with his porcine body set on long, delicate legs, and his great curved tusks, for which no man has found a reason,

[1] Wallace says probably to the Continent of Asia, but I heard scientists discussing Africa as possibly being the Continent.

[2] Cynopithecus nigrescens found also in Batchian.

[3] Babirusa found also in Bouru.

THE BABI-RUSA OR HOG-DEER.

THE ANOA DEPRESSICORNIS OR SAPI-UTAN.

To face page 128.

though the ancients thought that he hung upon trees with them and so rested and slept !

Curious it is that the naturalists of ancient days knew of the " four-horned hog," though he has never existed save in Celebes, and another island of the East. The horns are in verity not horns but tusks, and are of ivory, without trace of enamel. The boar alone has these tusks, the canines of the sow being small. The upper tusks curve backwards and even pierce the skin of the face, the lower ones are too long and too curved to be of any use as teeth. Surely the babirusa must use them in fighting for the sow. When she has young, she hides them for a few days in a hole lined with leaves, but her young seldom number more than two at a birth. The Malay word " babirusa " means pig-deer, and indeed at a distance, its graceful form recalls a deer rather than a pig.

Squirrels and opossums complete the mammals. Besides these are seven strange varieties of bats; and out of one hundred and eighteen kinds of butter-flies, eighty-six kinds spring only from Celeban soil—some are swallow-tailed; all are beautiful.

How wonderful is the maternity of Celebes—fecund in beings that live only there, and that belong, perhaps, to a former era of the earth.

CHAPTER II

THE ISLAND OF BALI

" Dear are the names of home

.   .   .   .

But we have tasted wild fruit, listened to strange music ;
And all shores of the earth are but as doors of an inn.
We knocked at the doors and slept ; to arise at dawn and go."

LAURENCE BINYON.

I CANNOT bear to say anything of Ceylon, Singapore, or even of Java, places that were but prefaces to the real journey.

To see the blessed sun, that was good ! It was amusing, too, to be on a veteran ship. On her ample deck we sat down to a generous board, feasting on good foods, whilst our eyes shone with pleasure to see the dancing waves.

The sea was too contrary for the *Swaedercroon* to ship any merchandise from the port of Boeleleng, but we took a native canoe and made for the shore, though we were doubtful about being able to land, so great was the surf.

Hurled by the foaming waves on to the shores of Bali, we had, though we knew it not, reached one of the most fantastic places of the earth.

Bali is too near Java for security from the blight of European ugliness that will fall upon it; it is now like the dream of an opium eater.

"AND THEY PRAY."

To face page 130.

I remember best the white ibis—the flights of ibis at sunset; also the great bulls of Bali, with their brown hides, and the patch of white near the tail. They seemed aloof, noble, atavistic. They came from a jungle stock; some wild ones are said still to exist. The fields are ploughed by them. Once a year they are ornamented with a great bell, and with fine adornment, then they race against each other, and are garlanded with flowers. They are cherished by the people.

The people. What of them ?[1]

They are the darlings of the Dutch. No missionary may live in Bali. The Dutch glory in having this Hindu people under their mantle, uniquely Hindu, for all the other " Indians " honour the Prophet, or Christ, or are merely heathen. These men of Bali came from Java about 1400 A.D., led by princes from Majapahit.

In Bali shrine after shrine is built to Hindu gods. These temples in red sandstone are works of beauty, the stone blossoming into flowers. The portals to the courts of the shrines and the temples themselves are, alas, perishable.

Behind these carved portals there are girls, beautiful girls, with long hair, and wearing yellow flowers. They carry armfuls of flowers and incense, and they pray. They smiled to me; they gave me flowers destined for their altars. The Armenian with us had lived there many years; he could not leave Bali. " He has drunk of guna-guna," I was told, " of the

[1] When Raffles lived we fought against them ; that was in 1814.

draught that the Bali women prepare that bewitches a man."

Our bewitched friend took us everywhere, and the women, knowing him, did not trouble to veil their bosoms when he passed. I can never forget them, these women of Bali. They walked like queens, hundreds of them, along the fine smooth roads. They carried on their heads baskets with rice and fruit; their nether garment was of silk, or of a fine fabric. Above it they wore a scarf of drawn work, and their rounded breasts lay open to the sun. Talbot said that in all his long travels he had never seen women like these—never seen so many in the open road, never seen women working and remaining splendid, upright, statuesque. Years ago widows were burned in the great fires of the dead, but the last to be consumed followed her lord along the fiery way in 1903.

The Balinese are, I believe, cruel, but they know how to die, and when to die.

Did I not see the cross-road where, in 1908, Dewa-Agong and his wives with their children, thirty or forty people, came out before the Dutch soldiers. They were defeated, they could fight no more; their lovely hand-wrought swords were powerless against guns, so they stood in the road, and they cast in front of the blue-eyed soldiers jewels and silks. "Take these, but shoot us first," they cried. The men of Holland could not do that, so, amid the jewels and silks in the dust of the road, the royal men and women killed their children and then they stabbed themselves.

Photograph by Violet Clifton.

BALI GIRL CARRYING A COCONUT.

To face page 132.

The epic of the island is the beauty of the earth and the fostering industry of the people.

The people have associations or " subaks " which control the land in well-defined districts, and each has its own water supply. The " subak " also enacts rules as to the planting and the possessing of the land. It governs the care of animals, and is arbitrator in disputes between the owners of the various " sawas " or rice fields.

In 1914, about a hundred and thirty-six thousand acres of sawas were irrigated by running water, which is cunningly applied to the undulating land by means of reservoirs, waduks, aqueducts and drains.

The men of Bali have evolved this system by themselves. As farmers and engineers they excel.

They also enjoy themselves.

Being favoured by the Dutch, they are allowed to have cock-fights, for they do not waste their substance on betting as do the Sumatrans.

The music of Bali is the crowing of cocks. Everywhere in the villages the men eat together at a common board, whilst the cocks, each in his wicker cage, crow defiance and await the contest. Now I learned the meaning of " the white feather," for I noticed that cocks with white feathers were dastardly and shook and fretted before the fight. The cocks are armed with blades, some four inches long, sharp as razors, and one blow kills. I saw nothing cruel in the sport, death being immediate.

The peak of Bali is the supreme beauty of the island. It rises 10,497 feet, lending dignity to the sawas, where in the lowlands the rice is nearly golden, whilst in the terraced lands above the crop is still tenderly green.

The villages are gloomy, walled-in and dirty ; lean dogs prowl about, dogs that none may kill, because, maybe, the soul of an ancestor dwells therein. No man may kill the dog, but all men may kick him, and "there goes somebody's father," said Talbot, as an unhappy cur went screaming down a lane.

Among the beauties of Bali were the sculptured baths. There was an enclosed court where the women delighted in the water that came out of bamboo spouts. These even the bewitched man did not dare to approach. Therefore I went alone. Near by was the men's bathing court. Beyond this, in the open, little mares and stallions were, in their own court, washed and cooled by the spurting water.

We lived in a Rest House at Singaradja. Dutch travellers were there. Bali, with its good roads attracting others, was not remote enough for Talbot.

We sailed for Celebes.

BALI GIRLS CLOTHED FOR A RELIGIOUS PROCESSION.

WEAVING.

Photograph gift of Mr. Edgar.

To face page 134.

CHAPTER III

GOING NORTH

' . . . . We sailed to win ;
Only a wider sea ; room for the winds to blow,
And a world to wander in."

L. BINYON.

WE stopped in Macassar. Mr. Arathoon, the
Armenian who served as British Consul, saved us from
the hotel to which we had gone. He took us into his
own house, and to him be thanks for ever.

Afterwards we sailed north to Menado, the Explorer the while evolving a plan. Menado is as pretty
a town as there is east or west. The sea laps about it,
and fishes swarm near the shore, leaping and shimmer-
ing in the sun. The trees are noble ; noble, too, are the
ancient Portuguese walls and fortresses. Orchids
grow in the gardens, and bougainvillea and hibiscus.
The houses of the colonists are of the old type, modelled
on native houses, and having great, cool, delightful
thatches that slope down nearly to the ground. I had
fever in Menado—an elating fever, the kind that sets
you on a pinnacle, high up somewhere above your
body. The sleep afterwards was ample recompense
for any suffering—that long sleep on the camp bed in
the hotel gardens under the palms, the deepest, most

135

wonderful, most resting sleep that ever encompassed me.

We wanted to fish. No one but the natives ever fished, but we got a dug-out and some fishermen and went on the glaring sea. I remember that I was very hot, that I wore thick khaki, as the sun would have blistered me had I worn thin clothes. I was a blemish on the landscape.

I saw a white man in pyjamas on the beach, and all I had ever heard of beachcombers swarmed into my mind. Seizing Talbot's arm, I entreated him to adopt the Westerner, to salve him from this beach, and from the drunken men of Sangi who surrounded him.

" He is an albino," came the soothing assurance.

Whilst at Menado, Talbot saw the Talaud group of islands marked upon a map. It lies north of Celebes, north even of the Sangi group, and he heard that it was but little known and visited by a steamer only once a month. He heard, too, that it was reported to be unhealthy and certainly a locality to avoid. It became a place of instant possibilities. Deep sea fishing might reveal monster fish, the people could not fail to be original, and certainly we must go there. So, through the usual barrage of official advice to the contrary, we went.

The Resident of Menado, who had wished, solely for our own sakes, to prevent our going to Salibaboe Island, the main isle of the Talaud group, very kindly gave us a letter commending us to the care of the native ruler. Therefore, provisioned with a little of the Malay language, which is the language of the headmen of the islands, with our servant Ambrose (whittled down to 'Bros), our camp beds and some foodstuffs, we sailed away on our two and a half days' journey on the s.s. *Shouten*. The skipper was Captain Van den Blink, who in six years had commanded thirty different steamers cruising amid the Dutch Indies.

The next day we tarried at Taroena, the port of Great Sangi Island. The island looked like a bouquet of coconut palms. It has a burning volcano in the centre, and a people so idle as to be content to wait for the coconuts to fall from the palms and then merely to ship away the valuable parts of the fruit. It is said that whilst the nuts are ripening the men of Sangi do nothing at all except sing hymns ; for they are Christians ! Idyllic as this may sound, when the nuts do fall, the curse of Adam can no longer be evaded, for the preparation of the copra for export is arduous.

We landed a large company of men who were returning from Menado after a drinking bout of a fortnight's duration. The men of Sangi have a passion for drink and become mad when intoxicated, therefore no strong spirits are allowed in this group of islands. These Malays of Sangi are separated from their bliss by twenty-four hours of seafaring ere they can reach Menado, but when they do accomplish the journey they enjoy a long carousal. For only once every fourteen days does the steamer revisit Sangi.

The whistle was blowing its last warning when a Dutch missionary came on board, and on deck wrote a long letter. The captain waited till he had closed it, then the old man left the steamer and was rowed back to Taroena, where he had lived for twenty-five years. He was very nervous, very ill ; and this matter of a letter to be written on every outgoing steamer was his " idée fixe."

He instructed the native children and held services for the adults. But he was poor, and had not enough to do. He was indeed flotsam on that sorry island.

We were the only first-class passengers, except some Chinese traders who cruise between the islands buying dried coconut husks.

On the morning of the third day anchor was lowered in the Bay of Liroeng, the port of Salibaboe.

CHAPTER IV

SALIBABOE

"I shook the tree of knowledge, ah ! the fruit
    Was fair upon the blackness of the soil,
    I filled a hundred vessels with my spoil,
And then I rested from the grand pursuit."
THE DIWAN OF ABU'L-ALA.

ACCOMPANIED by Captain Van den Blink and by our servant 'Bros, we landed, carrying a loaf of ship's bread, a piece of beef, a block of ice, and our letter to the native Chief. The dark Djoejoejoe, Witmanoe, was waiting at the landing, dressed in a white drill suit. His boots were brightly polished, and his teeth, filled with gold, were gleaming in the sunshine His official cap was embroidered with a " W "—for Wilhelmina, the Queen of the Netherlands ; on his buttons, too, was " W " beneath a crown.

He read the letter, and told the Captain that the official Rest House was in ruins, but that he would welcome us into his own house.

We entered the Djoejoejoe's house, a pretty building like a European bungalow, with " Villa Theodora " painted in large letters on the façade.

The s.s. *Shouten* soon sailed away. Willy-nilly we must remain here for a month. The Chieftain gave us his own room, which had a very hard wooden bed with a mosquito net, a wash-stand, a few nails to hang clothes on, a concrete floor and wooden walls. The room had glass windows. Just outside grew a wonderful hibiscus plant, outlined against the fiery blue of the sky. We put our camp beds in the verandah, then went to an inner room to lunch on tinned beef and rice with tinned fruit, whilst Maria, the cook, and Paulina, a friend of hers, fanned us with leaves to keep the flies away. The bathing place and the kitchen lay beyond this room. The kitchen was revolting, with dogs and flies and the frying of half-hatched eggs. Because of all this disorder, I seldom had the courage to cook, but sometimes I tried to teach Maria.

When we had been in Liroeng for the space of eight days she taught me to make bread, using coconut water as a ferment in place of yeast. The bread was very good.

For a few days I hated Liroeng. The flies disgusted me, and the Djoejoejoe was as yet no friend of mine. He was to me but a dark, coarse, sweaty person, disgusting with boils. Later on I liked the wit and temper of the man.

The hot, fly-blown, empty first days passed, then, after hating it, suddenly I enjoyed this place where our life was farcical. We seemed to be living in an operetta by Gilbert and Sullivan. I will ring up the curtain on some of the scenes in the chapters that follow.

THE DJOEJOEJOE AND THE NOÑA.

CHAPTER V

THE PIG HUNT

*" And all the day they hunted,
And nothing could they find
But the moon a-gliding
A-gliding with the wind."*

Nursery Rhyme.

A-HUNTING we would go, for we knew that the wild pig of the island are large and fine, descendants, it is said, of English porkers that had fled to the jungle from a ship wrecked upon the coast. Before we could start on the destined day, we had to listen to a surfeit of hymns, for nearly every morning those lazy people sang to us countless religious songs. The men made a fine group, but the women were ugly, with dull eyes. School children came too, with flags and flutes and a drum, and a little tinkling bell that marked the time for them. They were summoned to school with a booming call sounded on a conch shell; but first they sang to us. On this hunting day they unduly delayed us, but at last we went off to a village three miles away, the heathen village of the island. The " great lord," the Resident of Menado, had, in a letter, entrusted us to the care of the Djoejoejoe, Witmanoe, who was too careful of us. Over anxious, he prevented our going into the jungle. Instead he sent men with long spears

141

and pariah dogs to drive wild pig towards some open ground, near the village, where Talbot could get a shot; therefore our part was to go to the village and to await the expected sounder of pig.

We walked along a white coral road that dwindled into a path, bordered with sea pinks; behind the tufts of flowers were bamboo fences, beyond which lay the thatched bungalows of the people. The first Comptroller had these flowers planted before the Dutch Government put the island into the charge of the Native Ruler. They remained to mark the lasting blessing of a passing lover of flowers.

The heathen village was a lovely place. Every house was surrounded by palms and by pineapples. Each house had a Dutch flag flying. Men came bowing and calling out a welcome from the lintel of every gate-post, and at the end of the village we were greeted by " Captain of the Sea." This euphonious title is bestowed on the headman of each village. The Captain now bade us enter his house. He shook hands with me, as did his wife with Talbot; and this was an honour, because for them it was sinful to hold the hand of a person of the opposite sex; but they broke their own code that they might prove their amity.

The house was beautifully built of forest wood, and far surpassed in worth and handicraft that of the Djoejoejoe. The chairs and tables had been fashioned out of teak and ebony by workers of the village. Modern German pictures hung upon the walls. There was a picture of the Czar and the Czarina, and another

THE HUNTING PARTY.

Photographs by J. Talbot Clifton.

" THE WILD PIG ARE LARGE AND FINE."

To face page 142.

of the Awakening of Brunhilda. Strangest of all was one depicting a vision of Gerhardt Hauptmann, which here gave a strangely exotic feeling.

The men of the village worked very much harder than those of Liroeng, and the Djoejoejoe never had to punish them for neglect of their land or of their houses. The workmen, like those of Liroeng, were dressed in pyjamas, and the " dandies " wore white European suits; save the Captain of the Sea who was in deep blue. A few only of the men wore the pretty Javanese batik cloth fashioned into trousers.

Two flaxen haired children walked into the verandah. " Some European has been here before us," murmured Talbot; but we were told that the children were albinos, much prized for their fairness. The usual family of Salibaboe numbers the Malthusian four, but the mother's ignorance often causes the death of two or three. The island mothers are generally unable to suckle their young, which curious fact is, I surmised, due to lack of stamina caused by interbreeding.

We lunched whilst we waited. Lovely birds were brought to us. The first was a pigeon twice the size of an English wood-pigeon, with a snow-white body, night-black tips to its wings, and a buff-coloured head. The next was leaf green, with red feathers under the wings. After that a megapode was laid before us.

Later in the afternoon when we had returned to the Villa Theodora, quivering with eagerness, I sought to classify this handsome bird by reading the various descriptions of megapodes and of the kindred " maleo " which Wallace gives in his book on the Malay Archipelago. We had seen megapodes in the Nicobar Islands, but they were merely brown, and hen-like, whereas this fine bird had bands of chestnut brown upon its back and wings. The megapodes of the Nicobars had built with their strong feet great mounds of sticks and leaves. But the species I was studying burrows obliquely two and a half feet or more into the sand. There the female lays puce-coloured eggs, so big that she faints after ejecting them ! At least so the Djoejoejoe told me. One egg from such a bird sufficed to make an omelette for both of us.

I found that Wallace had discovered in the Moluccas a species of megapode that has been named *Megapodius Wallacei*. The description of this bird tallied with that of the megapode before me.

The next trophy to be brought in to us as we waited in the heathen village was a tree lizard over three feet long. Now we began to see that this hunt was a fictitious one. We were told that two dogs had been badly wounded by an enormous tusker. In truth, the curs had fought one another, but on their wounds was based this fable. We were now assured that the pigs had fled back into the jungle. " In that case we had better return," said Talbot. Whereupon the Djoejoejoe said : " Yes, we will send for the beaters," and in a few minutes' time they came forth from obvious hiding places. We were annoyed at being considered so simple, but understood both then and afterwards that we were like state prisoners, and that, lest any

THE PORTALS OF BALI.

To face page 144.

mishap might befall us, we should never be allowed
any kind of adventure or even freedom. As a peace
offering the Captain of the Sea shot a wild pig during
the night, and for some days we had fresh pork.

CHAPTER VI

LIFE IN LIROENG

"I had a little nut-tree, nothing would it bear
But a silver nutmeg and a golden pear ;
The King of Spain's daughter came to visit me,
And all was because of my little nut-tree.
I skipped over water, I danced over sea,
And all the birds in the air couldn't catch me."

Nursery Rhyme.

THE sea and seashore—in these we found enchant-
ment. To bathe every morning and every evening in
the liquid lapis lazuli—that was sheer delight. To
run along the sands in the moonlight—that, too, was
good. Under coconut palms I went nightly, and beneath magnolia trees, past flowering mangroves which
gave out a heavy alluring perfume. Great white
lilies reflected the silver of the moon, and with sweet,
overpowering scents they called to the nocturnal moths
to bestow fruitfulness upon them. Little nutmeg
trees grew laden with fruits like the nuts of the nursery
rhyme.

In charge of the Captain of the Sea, we several times
went out fishing. The currents were swift, the sea
ran fast and deep, and save for some garfish, green
boned, with teeth like a saw, and a few mullet, we got
nothing. The method of our going was pleasant.

First there was the solemn parting with the Djoejoejoe, who charged the lively and picturesque Captain of the Sea with our safety, then came the singing of hymns around the house, and then down to the boat came a child dipping the Dutch flag. Afterwards the flag was entrusted to a man in the boat, whose sole charge was to hold it while eight other men rowed us. The Captain *di Laut* steered, and once away on the sea we encouraged the men to sing. As they got to know us better they would often break out into their old war songs, and their aforetime heathen and cannibal recitatives. When Witmanoe was with us he made a feint of discouraging this; then the oarsmen would suddenly lapse back into such foreign airs as " The Last Rose of Summer."

I learned much while rowing and fishing. I was told that the Djoejoejoe punished his people by making them work for us. If the natives failed to keep their gardens tidy, if their houses were not well thatched, or if they failed to salute us humbly, they were punished. " Are we men of the jungle that we should live in bad houses, or fail to tend the earth, or are we savages that we should shed our coats ? " So reasoned Witmanoe. I once pleaded the cause of some men who had laid aside their pyjama tops when they were working, but he would not forgive them. " We have never been a naked people," he said, and Mussolini-like he forced on each wrong-doer a large dose of unpleasant medicine. " If you feel the heat so much, you must be ill," he grumbled. His energy was as great as their inertia, his eyes were as enkindled as theirs were dull. He had silver spoons, and table cloths ; and if Holland is clean, why, so is Salibaboe !

I learned that sympathy is a sentiment entirely lacking in Orientals, a discovery which, once made, was later confirmed in a hundred ways and places. This seems to me to be one of the main differences between the East and the West. Or is it the difference between the Christian and the non-Christian ; or is it— most of all—the difference between the modern and the mediaeval outlook ? Sympathy is very modern, for in the old days only the Saints were compassionate.

Several times I said : " Are not the men tired with rowing, Captain of the Sea ? Shall we not drift a little now ? " He would shout at the men : " The lady sees you pull so badly that she thinks you must be tired. Pull harder, or I will strike you." He could not understand what I had intended.

Once the water rushed into our boat, for the wind and tide were contrary, and the waves were very high. A man baled for an hour, and went on baling until at last I took a coconut shell and stooped to help him. Instantly my movement was misunderstood. " Work quicker. See the lady has to help you, lazy idler," yelled the Captain of the Sea.

Though there were neither horses nor asses upon this island, yet some bulls and cows were kept; I do not know for what purpose, as fresh milk was not used. One of the bulls was a great gentle beast of the kind seen in Bali, beautiful as Jupiter seeking Europa, but he was covered with sores, and infected by jungle insects. I bathed his sores and persuaded our Chief

148

Photograph by J. Talbot Clifton.

BROS WITH A MEGAPODE.

to let him pasture in some long grass near the house, where we could watch him, and could easily attend him. I tried to impress the Djoejoejoe with the needless torment the animal endured by being driven into the dense places near the village, and to prove how easily he could be healed.

Then Paulina's leg broke out into a sorry sore. I doctored it and made it clean and wholesome. It needed care that it might heal. We went away for a few nights—of that more anon—and returned to find that Paulina had taken off the bandages, walked about, and reopened the sore. She had tried to make amends by such free use of my precious unguents that hardly any were left. The leg was poisoned, and I found a terrifying sore where I had left a clean one. She had also dug out the pus with a rusty pin ! Furiously I sought the Djoejoejoe, recited my discovery, and told him he must order Paulina to tend her knee. " Itoe busuk ? " he asked, unmoved. I did not know the latter word, but in a dictionary found, " rotten and stinking." So he had asked : " Is it rotten and stinking ? " I understood, then, how very definite, tangible and visual a hurt must be to impress these casual children of the sun. Far from medical skill and care, perhaps it is well that only desperate cases should arouse anxiety in their minds. So, by land and on sea, I learned to understand a little the Djoejoejoe and his subjects.

CHAPTER VII

THE NONA

> " For there is ample room for bliss
> In pride in clean brown limbs,
> And lips know better how to kiss
> Than how to raise white hymns."
> COUNTEE CULLEN.

OH Salibaboe ! What a strange memory you are, with your coral road and your sea pinks and your one bond with the outer world—the mighty coconut palms! As for us, we had in Salibaboe no freedom, no privacy. I have understood since being there the martyrdom of royal persons, the torment of their daily lives. Until my hours were subjected to the watchful eyes of the people of Salibaboe, I did not know what a shirt of Nessus watching eyes can be. When we walked abroad to some of the further villages, the people, using as medium the Djoejoejoe, would importune us to show ourselves. They wanted nothing else, they never asked for money or for gifts, but they walked miles and miles just to see us, just to be allowed to sit all day staring through us. That meant goodbye to solitude, even to what we consider decency, for in most of the houses there were no shutters, no glass windows, and, with spectators round the dwelling, I could neither change nor wash without being seen. As for liberty, the farcical episode of the hunt had proved that we were considered too precious to be lightly exposed even to fatigue.

One day we left Liroeng to see another village. " Come and visit the Nona," said our host.

The Nona was the daughter of the ruler of a neighbouring island, and was the childless widow of yet another ruler. She remains in my mind with a background of coconut palms and of singing natives.

We started forth with Witmanoe and a few men, who, as a punishment, were made to carry the luggage. We walked some miles. Suddenly we were met by a crowd of men and boys. They came towards us carrying palm-branches, flags and banners. Blowing on shrill flutes and pipes, and beating large drums, they saluted us. After we had greeted them, they walked behind us playing as they went. They loved us for being white.

I regretted my unattractive looks. In short khaki clothes with puttees and a large felt hat, my face crimson with heat, I was not an inspiring figure ; but Talbot is always impressive. The people, however, seemed to like the look of us.

We reached the Nona's house, cool with its large verandah, and built near a river. The little lady, in Malay clothes, gave us tea in fine Japanese cups, and delicious cakes which she herself had baked.

She was charming, olive skinned and gracious. The gentle assurance of her princely blood became her well. Her background was formed of her greatest possessions—her china and her palms. The verandah was hung with plates, and ornamented with bowls and vases from China that blossomed with flowers and colours: blues, deep pinks, and most entrancing greens. Often in the villages we were tantalized with such pottery, beautiful, and, I am sure, valuable; but no one ever wished to sell, and we would not allow the Djoejoejoe to insist. The Nona wanted to give us some pieces, but we would not accept. It is pleasant now to think of this china being still in Salibaboe, the one thing of art and culture that is there. It is the price that was paid some hundred years ago for slaves. The people think that the china is Spanish, but I know it to be Chinese. It was the medium of barter for slaves between the islands; probably Chinese traders sailed here bringing pottery and taking away human beings to sell elsewhere. The china was exchanged against broken lives, tears, blood and separation; now it is above price; it cannot be bought. The human beings who were bartered for it are dead: it remains most beautiful. Did the island lose or gain by its ancient trading? A haunting question; like the absurd one: "Which would you save in a fire, an old woman or a glorious work of art?"

Behind the house stood the tall palms, green and fruitful here; source of wealth to the little lady who was giving us tea. She was threatened by fate. Her fortune stood in jeopardy, for in many of her plantations the palms hung black and ugly, their leaves pierced and darkened by a terrible insect pest.

The other cloud that overhung our hostess was her indecision in response to the Djoejoejoe's ardent suit.

I think that he cared for her ; certainly he desired her, and by her wealth and position, probably also by her culinary skill, was tempted to marry her speedily. But the Nona was a good Christian ; she had been educated by missionaries. They wrote to her, influencing her always against our Chief ; for he had another wife. He told me that she had been cruel to him, but later on I heard otherwise. She had gone to live in Menado, and I suppose he was divorced. The Nona was troubled. When I knew her, fate loomed darkly before her, perplexing her. Soon after we had left the island, she married the Chief ; two years later she died.

Whilst we were resting, some cousins of the Djoejoejoe came in, with a small dark infant, asking if they might name it Talbot Clifton, which boon was granted them. Some English traveller—years hence—meeting this lad, and knowing of our journey to Salibaboe, may think uncharitably of his parentage.

Restored and rested, we now turned homewards, escorted by our musicians. I spent the evening laboriously preparing, for the following day, my conversation with the Djoejoejoe, having many words to learn in Malay, before I could frame the questions I had in mind to ask him. The study was rendered more difficult by the night's revelry, for Witmanoe gave a dance. The musicians were two Chinese, one of whom played the drum whilst the other tortured a violin. For their refreshment a delicious fruit cup was first offered to the guests, and later some brandy, a present from the Explorer, was consumed by the company in very small and discreet quantities. The women could not dance fast owing to their loose sandals ; the men had heavy shoes or boots. The dances chosen were waltzes and polkas, and the music went on and on monotonously all night, the big drum beating the time. The Nona came and danced in spite of her regard for the Missionary, who next Sunday, in the schoolhouse used as a church, declaimed against the sin of dancing. He did not even like to see a man and woman walking down the street together.

We sought our beds on the verandah whilst revelry held sway in the room behind. My last impression of the night was the sight of the Djoejoejoe joyfully rubbing his hands and saying : " Plaisir, plaisir ; whilst I am Chief of the island that is what I will have ; all that I want is plaisir." [1]

[1] "The Malay language did not, apparently, contain a word to express his desire as well as did the European word "Plaisir," and again "plaisir."

CHAPTER VIII

A NIGHT ON THE HILL

"But it is surmised he was British, for the reason that
the people of that nation like to do what is disagreeable to
them and glory in their vigour."

Japanese Judgment on one who climbed
a Holy Hill in Japan.

SOME ONE once defined the simple people as compared
to the gentle as "the unconscious classes"—an
adequate definition. The people of Salibaboe are
very unconscious. They do not know their past
history, nor have they any tribal distinctions; what they
remember of their tradition shocks them. Their
heathen songs are nearly forgotten, their heathen
dances they have exchanged for the waltz and the
lancers. At present this island people has but little
personality, and several generations must pass away ere
it evolves a definite character, builded on its new
creed and Western learning.

The only ancient monuments in Salibaboe are some
tombs near the sea, wherein are laid the forefathers
of the Djoejoejoe. I think they are not more than two
hundred years old. They are formed of dark massive
stones, and one of them is decorated with the effigy of
a crocodile. The tombs are very beautiful, surrounded with coconut palms; the immensity of the

sea lies beyond them. Of the graves of the lesser islanders I saw no trace ; they must have been consigned to the effacing earth without a stick or a stone to cry " Remember me ! "

Like little tunes remembered are some scenes from our opera-bouffe life in Salibaboe.

One day whilst I was admiring Paulina, who was seated on a grave, Witmanoe, who loved our roving ways, said : " Let us spend a night on the hill top." I assented, and he arranged our wayfaring. It was partly punitive, for he summoned all the men he wanted to chastise to be the carriers of the luggage.

He said : " These men have not grown the five hundred banana trees which it is decreed the head of every family shall own, for no man here may be a burden to the community because he lacks the food he should grow. These others are guilty because they built their houses rudely with rough bamboos instead of solidly with wood."

Shamefacedly, one took the kettle and the pans, the others our camp beds and food. The Djoejoejoe ordered four women to come with us. The Nōna also came, to be with me, as she liked me well, and I liked her. We had an exhausting ascent which took us an hour and a half. Witmanoe, who was dressed as we were, in practical khaki, went up on all fours, so that the Nona could pull herself up the hill by his coat. By this chivalry I saw that Christianity had flowered in his soul. The other women were exhausted and rather angry at having been made to come, but on the

"PAULINA SEATED ON A GRAVE."

Photograph by Violet Clifton.

To face page 156.

summit we soon all revived. We drank cold tea and ate tinned fruits in a swept-out compound beneath the hut, which hut was composed of but one room. This single room was built high on stakes, it was open at two sides, below it was the square shaded compound with a bamboo seat running round it.

Wild pig, and aroe leaves, which are used as vegetables, are the products of these hills. The natives used the hut when in search of either food.

The Djoejoejoe had had a sucking pig taken up. It was stuffed and roasted whole, picturesquely barbecued on a bamboo above the fire. Rice was folded into big leaves and boiled in green parcels for the men. We ate first, then ascended, and lay on our camp beds, out of the way whilst the others feasted. Our upper room was fitted rather for dwarfs than for big heavy Europeans, and our beds nearly broke through the reed floor on to the men who were eating under the hut.

The Nona and the Djoejoejoe and some others now retired to another small building a little way off. Towards evening the Explorer took his gun and we started off to see if we could find some wild duck on the lake above us.

One of our escort sounded an alarm to notify the Chief that his state prisoners were escaping, but Talbot silenced the alarmist.

We did not find any duck, but we saw a most lovely grove of bamboos and some tall lilies many feet high amid the thick tangle of the jungle.

As we retraced our steps we met the Djoejoejoe and most of the men coming out to seek us. They looked very miserable when Talbot jeered at them, saying, " Yes, the lake is very pretty.   Go and look at it ; " so they had to go on whilst we returned to the hut.

I was delighted at being rid of the escort, for, with only four " Peeping Toms " left, I was able to change into a tea gown, though I kept my leggings as the mosquitos were maddening.   Soon the many re-turned, and the Explorer called out to them : " I am going to change my clothes," but as they, both men and women, remained seated outside in full view of us, he proceeded to wash and change in front of them.

The sunset from the height was wonderful.   The sea and the distant island shone gold, red and purple ; above us flew to roost birds as brilliant as the sky.   Red paroquets went past, and green pigeons, then suddenly all colour was blotted out.   Night fell abruptly like a curtain let down at the end of a play.

Some of the men tried to sleep on the reed mats which they had brought, but the mosquitos swarmed in such legions that the women spent most of the night sitting on the hillside singing hymns.   We were often bitten in spite of our mosquito nets.   The Nona had the room in the other hut, and in his clothes, the Djoejoejoe slept there too, half hanging out of the room.   Whenever I woke up I could see his booted legs dangling over the open side of the room.   Next morning I dressed, hiding myself amid the enormous leaves of the aroe, and then descended the wet slippery pig path.   I found the descent as difficult as the ascent had been, but the other women tripped down easily. All four of them had malaria after this night on the hill, and the Nona too retired to her bed. I alone, though tired, remained well in spite of the adventure.

CHAPTER IX

KABOROAN

"Is happiness a solid thing
  Like gold, like ceremonial gear,
  That still you say 'I will possess it?'
A king of fruit, a clustering
  Of grapes, that yields a liquid cheer
  Instorable, if you shall press it?"

D. A. C. ANDRADE.

IN the person of Talbot the prophecies of the Resident of Menado were being fulfilled. The sixth plague of Egypt fell upon him; he suffered greatly with boils.

Witmanoe now offered to take us to Kaboroan, a small island lying to the south-east, where another Chief had sway. Ten men rowed us there. Landing, we were surprised to see but few coconut palms. This isle was a veritable garden of nutmeg trees that had been planted in the years when spices were of great value. The crop was now of little worth, though it gave Kaboroan a fairy-like appearance, covered as it was with this shining tree. Tidy bamboo hedges and masses of palms and hibiscus framed the coral paths. It would have been great happiness to embroider these lovely nut trees, to copy in finest yellow silks their small blossoms, to reproduce in long stitches the peach-coloured oval fruit surrounded by glossy leaves. When the fruit splits open to the sun it reveals a rich brown nut within, and the fruit has an inner coating, the crimson mace.

The houses with their long, sloping straw roofs were more beautiful than those of Liroeng. For the rest, the religion, the schools, and the clothes of the people were the same in this lovely little island as in Salibaboe But where were the minstrels, the shrill fife and drum band, the songs and hymns, the long enfolding looks, the welcomes that gladdened us everywhere in Salibaboe ? These were entirely lacking. The Chief of the island had received a message from our Djoejoejoe that we were coming. He had left his verandah empty for us to camp in, and a reed hut had been prepared for our ablutions, but he and his family had fled into the jungle leaving only some rice for our feasting. Our boatmen had returned to Liroeng, for we had intended remaining three or four days in Kaboroan to visit the old graves of the former rulers, some of which I had seen by the side of the path as I walked up from the shore. "There are also," Witmanoe said, " the remains of a Portuguese village, and you may be able to buy some of the old china that you so covet." These, then, were the allurements, but because the Chief had gone we could not get men to guide us. That this lesser ruler should dare to treat us with such despite so angered the Djoejoejoe that we determined to leave on the morrow.

In the early morning the sulky headman returned and consented to lend us a boat and eighteen men to row. The day was windy and rainy, the boat, which was old and neglected, leaked dangerously in the stormy sea. For two hours and a half the men rowed and paddled. The wind and the tide were contrary, and great waves rose up in the narrows. The men sang ancient war songs and gave loud cries. Secretly I was afraid, but the journey was accomplished at last.

We landed on the friendly shores of Salibaboe, on the beach of Moronge, the capital of Salibaboe, where the Nona had her town house. The Captain of the Sea of Moronge had seen the boat approaching and met us, accompanied by other notabilities and a troop of some thirty schoolboys and young men carrying flags, flutes, a drum and a bell. They sang a hymn, and cried " Hallelujah " and " Hurrah," as they escorted us to the Nona's house, which she shared with the Captain of the Sea. We climbed a ladder into the upper verandah, and were given a charming bedroom with curtained beds draped with fresh muslin to serve as mosquito netting. The walls were made of palm, the floor and the ceiling were of wood and of dried palms, and the breezes blew through and round our room deliciously. We had fared meagrely, but our feasting now began. The Nona had directed her cook in the preparation of some savoury dishes of wild pig and of fish and fowl, with drinks of fruit juice and wine. The people of the village sat down in the street below, watching us all the time we stayed in Moronge, the space of four days. When I wearied of their looking, the cook said : " The people with great hearts rejoice in the rulers ! " A room wherein to wash

"MORONGE WAS A SADDENING VILLAGE."

To face page 162.

was quickly built on to the house, which had no other accessory ; but the jungle lay near. As we always had a crowd following us we were forced at times to scream to the onlookers : " Pergi, pergi " —" Go on, go on."

Talbot was much impressed with the brazen curiosity of the people of Salibaboe, for, in all the world, he had seen no folk metal-eyed as these.

The following day was Sunday. The conch shells gave forth long, calling notes. Services, teaching and hymn singing went on without ceasing till half-past one on Monday morning. The Missionary gave the people the Lord's Supper once a year at a long table ; bread and wine and prayers; the charge to each person was sixpence. All the islanders, excepting only the inhabitants of one village, had been Christian for nearly a hundred years, therefore they were very friendly to white people.

Moronge was a saddening village, and that in spite of the music. The impression it has left on me is a heraldic sable. The coconut palms that overhung us were black. Witmanoe said this was so because of the rain at night, but in truth it was disease that darkened them. Threatening canopies, they overhung the houses, whispering " ruin " as the leaves shook in the breeze. The village had many ancient tombs—not beautiful. They, too, were black. The town contained five hundred houses, and not one shop.

All Monday night the people of Moronge sat grouped in the streets, singing hymns. On Tuesday Talbot shot some teal, and on Wednesday we walked three miles, inspired by the fife and drum band, to a village called, like the island, Salibaboe. I was the first white woman ever to enter it, as also to visit some remarkable caves, where long ago the islanders had worshipped beasts as gods. Afterwards, in the sixteenth or early seventeenth century, conquering Spaniards turned the now bat-haunted caves into a church. Mass had been heard here by the explorers. I was the first woman from Europe to enter the caves, there to recall the heroic departed !

The people of the village were rich in lovely china, which dignified their simple lives.

In the cool of the evening we returned to the flesh-pots of the Nona.

CHAPTER X

GOOD-BYE TO SALIBABOE

"All day long and all night through
  One thing only must I do,
  Quench my pride and cool my blood,

. . . .

  Not yet has my heart or head
  In the least way realised
  They and I are civilized."
                    COUNTEE CULLEN, Negro.

OUR time in Liroeng was drawing to a close ; which
was well, as Talbot was almost clothed in bandages
owing to the boils.

We were ready to leave Salibaboe. We had
watched the young men playing football in wonderful
jockey-like colours ; we had made, besides, what was
to us an interesting discovery in natural history.
One afternoon the Djoejoejoe came to Talbot excitedly,
saying : " I have seen a crocodile go up that creek.
It will eat the poultry of the dwellers of the hill. I
entreat you to get your rifle and shoot it." He then
summoned some men to whom a punishment was due,
ordering them to go up one side of the creek, to enter
it high up and drive down the crocodile. This task
they sadly undertook, fearing Witmanoe more than
they did the crocodile. Talbot waited, expecting an
easy shot, for there was a stretch of sand lying between

the mouth of the creek and the sea; this the animal would have to cross. We expected to see it wriggling painfully over the dividing sandy space. Suddenly it emerged from the creek, and in spite of its short legs galloped towards the sea. At this critical moment Talbot's rifle jammed, and the creature disappeared into the water. It surprised us very much thus to learn that the females of the species are speedy animals. They are in the habit of going on shore to lay their eggs, but the males, being spared these journeys, can hardly move on dry land.

The Comptroller arrived from another island in a fine roofed-over boat two days before we left. He came to try cases of crime committed since his visit the year before. There were but few criminal cases, but the only serious offence was very terrible. A young man of Moronge had violated a child, and she was called in to answer questions. I was shocked by her calm indifference, her unabashed and callous answers to the Comptroller's gentle questioning. Her parents also seemed quite unmoved by the nauseating details, but the criminal was given a long term of imprisonment in Menado.

In Salibaboe was no overcrowding, no painful labour, no poverty. There was music and perfect order. Yet it has left no idyll in my mind. For thirty days we had lived with an uncultured Oriental and then this abhorrent crime seared my brain.

In the house of the Chieftain there were no books, but Talbot, as is his wont on a long journey, consorted with Shakespeare, and I had Dante and flaming John of the Cross, tropic souls to companion me.

We took a moving farewell of the Djoejoejoe, and later on sent him our photographs framed, a football, and a silver tea service for his wedding. He writes to me still. In his last letter he said : " Paulina has fever, and Maria is ill, but only with the usual woman's sickness. The sea waves break on the shore opposite my house and ask : ' Why do the English man and woman not come and bathe in us ' ? and the coral paths cry out, ' Why do their feet not press us any more ' ? "

Rejoicing in the mail which the steamer brought us from Menado, and in the ship's unsoiled linen, the fresh napery, the clean glass and the unchipped china, we sailed away from Liroeng to the sound of speeding music and to the singing of hymns.

CHAPTER XI

THE RETURN TO MENADO

" If ever he happened to gaze for an instant at the gold-
tinted clouds of sunset, he wished that they were real gold
and could be safely squeezed into his strong box."

N. HAWTHORNE.

OUR return journey to Menado took five days, because
we called at several ports that we had not touched
at before. There was on board a Chinese merchant
who wished to buy ebony, therefore the steamer went
from place to place picking up this beautiful timber.
Sharp as a dirk, I hold the memory of a lonely
Dutchman who lived in one of the villages near which
we anchored. He was poor and lived entirely alone.
He had speculated in ebony and had lost money. The
reviving trade must have filled him with hope. He
came alongside in a canoe, but did not board the steamer.
I wished that he had been invited to do so, but perhaps
he would have been too shy to accept. He was unshaven and dressed in batik trousers with a pyjama top.
He looked haggard.

The ports on the north-west coast of Celebes
differed in one way from the ports on the south-
east coast, indeed from those in every other part of
the world in which I have been. Usually when a
steamer anchors, sailing boats and rowing boats hasten
towards her like children to their mother, but here was

MACASSAR MAN. HEAD OF THE
CARGO WORKERS.

BUGIS BOY.

Photographs by J. Talbot Clifton.

CHRISTIAN BOY FROM MINAHASSA.
North Celebes.

JAVANESE BOY WITH BATIK HEAD-
COVERING.

none of that pretty commotion. There was so entire a silence and lack of stir that it seemed as though we rode at anchor in front of a hostile or of a plague-ridden port. The people were too lazy to bestir themselves, therefore boats were swung out, lowered from the davits and rowed to shore taking men to handle the copra or the ebony. The motor launch owned by the steamship company towed back the barges weighted with merchandise. A special crew of men is taken on board at Macassar to work in the ports of the lotus-eaters.

The entrance into Menado is very lovely; the encircling bay embraces a small island where an active volcano was alight. The bay was lively with the leaping of innumerable fish.

That Talbot might recover from the boils, we decided on going into the hills. In Menado we were helped by an Armenian from Baghdad, who, with his cousins, had a large firm in Menado and in other parts of Celebes. He acted as British Vice-Consul. He called himself English, but he could barely speak our tongue. I do not know what language he spoke in his home in Menado, whether Armenian or Arabic. He was very dark, nearly black, but was always telling us a tale of how he had been the first white man in some place on the coast and, as such, an object of the greatest curiosity! He helped us in the kindest way. He interested me because of his frank and total absorption in the problem of making money. He was in Menado to make money. In five years' time he expected to have amassed enough to be able to leave Celebes and

169

go to England. Or was it to Baghdad ? He allowed himself no pleasures, save only motoring; he never invited anyone to a meal in his house. " I am here to make money, not to spend it," he said. " Why do you not bathe," I asked, when I saw the lovely bay and the warm sea. " That would not enrich me," he answered gravely. He took a series of tickets for a cinema and contracted a feverish cold before the tickets were exhausted. " I felt very ill, and would have been better in bed, but of course I had to go each night, as I had paid for the tickets," he said. Another ticket for which he had paid was the cause of even greater trouble ; it was one taken from the Koninklijke Paketvaart Maatschappij for a journey to some port up the coast, whither he wished to go accompanied by his aunt. When they boarded the ship, they found that a cabin with four berths was the only one available, and that two Japanese men were installed in it. He went to the captain, saying that he and his aunt would retain the cabin, and that the two Japanese must sleep on the deck. The captain answered that the company's rules allow a lady to share a cabin with two or three men but not with one. " But she would object to several and would like one," answered the Vice-Consul. " Ask her." At last the two Japanese were put on deck and compensated, and he and his aunt shared the cabin.

After our return to Europe, I was sad to hear that this man, who had been a friend to us, had died just before the end of the years that he had set aside in Menado for the attainment of his desire.

CHAPTER XII

THE MINAHASSA

" To the ordinary Englishman this is, perhaps, the least known part of the Globe."

WALLACE, in *The Malay Archipelago*.

WE were now in the part of Celebes called the Minahassa, the northern Christian part, which has been Protestant for over one hundred years, and which is looked upon by the Dutch as the cradle of the most civilised people under their government in these Indies. These Malays know a great deal about agriculture. They are sent to teach the natives of mid-Celebes how to grow coffee and rice, also to tend the sick, as in Liroeng, where the little hospital was served by young men of the Minahassa. They also teach in various schools. They cultivate the land even as the Javanese do, but, unlike the Mahommedans of Java, they have a very great devotion to the Dutch, whom they treat as elder brothers. They never pass a Hollander or an official dwelling without lifting their straw hats. They would be punished if they did not bow. Though they all know the Dutch language, they rarely venture to address a Dutchman in his own tongue. " It is for us to know their language, not for them to have to speak ours," say the Netherlanders.

I recalled, in the Minahassa, what a British Governor in a distant Eastern country had said to us about the Christians of the Orient : " The Portuguese and Spanish were extremely politic to convert the natives whom they subdued ; it is the only way whereby our races can be consolidated with the people of Asia. If all our subjects were Christians, as are, for example, the Goanese, there would be far less of the Eastern question to contend with, and hatred would not be fanned by religious fanaticism."

It was in the Minahassa that, guided by the Vice-Consul, we had sought our servant 'Bros before we went to Liroeng. He lived in a village named Tondano, 2,500 feet above the sea. Sweetly scented flowers surrounded him, and the great Lake of Tondano lay spread out before him. His father was a farmer who owned some land and ploughed large rice-fields with straining buffaloes led by men who walked up to the thighs in water. He had a pleasant wooden house with European furniture. He made us welcome with sweet drinks and with fruits whilst we awaited the coming of 'Bros, who entered later with lithe and languid movements, rubbing his eyes. He had bare feet, and a loose white suit which was not unpicturesque. He had been sleeping. Later on we remembered this, for he was nearly always asleep. He seemed to be hardly human, so somnolent was he ! His father and mother spoke to him of his duties and on his prospects, before entrusting him to us. I felt how dramatic it was for this village lad to wake up one afternoon and come away with two English people, to share adventures, to see ships and the sea, jungles, ports, towns. He did not seem at all impressed by the strange ways of fate, but with his bundle of matting for a bed, a small pillow, and a gay little wooden box, he followed us in a semi-comatose state, leaving behind him for the first time his native village with its gardens, its pretty houses and its many school children in neat overalls. It seemed incongruous that this boy should, during our journeys, accommodate himself in Eastern fashion to sleeping anywhere, eating anything, and to squatting on the floor, although he had been brought up in a house with Western chairs and beds.

In the Minahassa is a cool mountain place called Rurukan. Thither by motor car we went. We had taken a three weeks' lease of an empty house that Talbot might recover, in the cool of the hills, from his affliction of boils before we essayed to hunt the anoa.

We were in a house on the very site of one wherein Alfred Wallace had lived. In his entrancing book, *The Malay Archipelago*, we read how he had delighted in his bathing place below the hill, just as we delighted in it, and that, as we did, he admired the tangle of wild fig trees, the palms and ferns, that grow near the mountain streams. I am wrong. His enjoyment of nature was sharpened by deep knowledge ; it was therefore greater than ours. His towering mind, feasting on the earth's manifestations and pondering the meaning of them, was, perhaps in this very Ruru-kan, groping towards the mighty theory of evolution which Darwin, working in England, was on the eve of making public.

Now in outline I shall tell you of this village amid the hills. We are 3,000 feet above sea-level, and the Klabat, noble volcano, rises 6,000 feet in our view, with its twin brothers outlined near it. It is evening. We have had the supper that I have cooked.

Up the hill into the village come the peasants returning from the fields below. They are of a pale yellow colour, tall and strong. Men and women walk together in unlovely clothes and wide straw hats. They yodel as they come ; at least I do not know how else to name their curious calling cries. " The ploughman homeward plods his weary way " is not true of their return. They do not salute or smile at us, but they yodel and sing all the way home. They have stable seasons, without threat of drought or of frost; they grow rice and maize, potatoes, coffee, cucumbers, oranges and bananas, and they tap the great sugar palm, the arenga saccharifera. Most beautiful of all palms, it yields abundant sugar and " sagueir," the wine of the palm, a drink which is to these people as cider to us.

Comfortable are their lives. Nearly a hundred years lie between their present well-being and the time when their forebears were head hunters always engaged in petty warfare. The Netherlanders and the missionaries can point to them with pride as a happy people weaned from savagery, reared to a prosperous independence by the system so well understood by the Dutch as paternal despotism.

SOMEBODY'S HOME IN BALIKH PAPAN.

Photographs by J. Talbot Clifton.

THE KLABAT AND A SUGAR PALM.

To face page 174.

They enter the village, which is quickly absorbed by the night. We see shining in the north the Great Bear, but we miss the Northern Star as we gaze on these constellations. Rose bushes and orange trees mix their perfumes with that of a small white orchid that grows a few feet from our house. The butterflies, as large as birds, disappear ; the bamboos rustle faintly and the owl hoots plaintively. Our lamp grows dimmer, the fireflies become more brilliant. We hear our boy call " Slamat tidor "—" Sleep well "—to a village maiden ; we go to our camp beds, whence we can see the stars. I lie looking at them, pondering the flavour of a fresh nutmeg fruit.

Then comes disillusionment. I remember that the village maiden is a leper, as are many of the people here. The silence of the night shivers into noise. This past day, every day, was horrid with unceasing noise. At dawn an unmelodious drum summoned the men of the village to meet the tuan or headman, who allotted the work, all the peasants being sent to one field or plantation which needed culture, for the work here is mostly communal.

All day children cried, cocks crowed, half-starved dogs howled, pigs squealed, badly oiled carts creaked, people chanted out of tune, yodeled, banged drums, and blew on conch shells. Never, in all the width of the world, have I heard such unceasing clamour. Now, in the night, the men go to visit their rat traps. They play drums and sing as they go, but a nearer commotion fills me with pity and disgust. The village dogs, loosed at last, are seeking food. They leap up the steps of our verandah, rush past our camp beds into the dining room, madly searching for food, like wild beasts, but bolder. They scramble up through the windows into the other rooms, then disappointed, they go elsewhere. To-night there is an added unrest, for in the late evening many ox-carts came creaking up the hill, and even now they continue to arrive. A white man or an Arab, or a Chinese, has come up to Rurukan to claim the mistress he has chosen. The man and the woman have appeared before the tuan. Now they are feasting in the house of the woman's parents. The man gives them a certain sum and is free to keep the woman for a year, or two years, and this will be well, as she will bring back some money to her parents' house. He may perhaps keep her till she has had eight or ten children and then marry her; if he be a Dutchman, he will almost certainly legalise the children as soon as they are born. Later, he will send them to Holland to be educated.

The noisy night grows silent. Sunday dawns. The Catholic school and then the other two schools summon their people with bells. I walk to the Catholic school, past the houses, now ornamented with the antlers of the mountain deer, as long ago they were ornamented with human skulls. No priest has come up this Sunday from the world below us, so only a few prayers are said. The people are devout. Among them I see two lepers, sitting freely among the others. " No one would like to thrust them away," I am told. The small boys respond in Latin, which sounds strange in these remote heights.

We found a teacher to help us with Malay, but he taught in such a way that we soon excused ourselves from further lessons. Though I plied him with questions he told us but little. He did tell me one thing that I have never forgotten; with the record of it, I shall end this chapter. It was the tale of a perfectly balanced day. "Early in the morning," he said, "I go to bathe in the place that you know on the hillside, afterwards I teach in the school till mid-day. Then I go home and eat, and rest a little, and later I work at my plantation, where I grow many vegetables ; this work is pleasure to me. After nightfall I take my books, and I read and study before I go to sleep."

CHAPTER XIII

MR. WANG

"During twelve years spent amid the grandest tropical vegetation, I have seen nothing comparable to the effect produced in our landscapes by gorse, broom, heather. . . ."
A. M. WALLACE.

TALBOT had recovered his health and his thoughts turned to shooting an anoa. We were told this animal lived in the northern part of Celebes, opposite the island of Limbe. A young Chinaman on the steamer from Liroeng had arranged that his uncle should receive us in his coconut plantation on the north-east of Celebes, so we travelled for three hours in a motor bus, from Menado on the west to Kema on the east, a distance of twenty-one miles.

The road was very ugly. Tin-roofed houses everywhere defiled the country. The men in a few of the hamlets were also repulsively ugly. They wore billy-cock hats and carried leather boots. They were dressed in heavy blue serge, as though they aped the fashion of sailors. At Kema I remember the pouring rain, and the all-absorbing eyes that encompassed us. We sat on the verandah of the Rest House waiting for the rain to cease before we should take a canoe to Mr. Wang's house in the Straits of Limbe. Natives stood in front of us and stared. They wore various kinds of clothing, and without emotion they looked at us for an hour or more. I longed to ask the men if they liked or disliked us, what were they thinking, what were they wondering, but my Malay was too weak for psychological discoveries. Whatever they might have answered had I questioned them, they would never have said they were interested in us, for in Malay there is, I think, no synonym for " interesting." When I told this to an author, he was not surprised, for " interest," he told me, is very modern, a word hardly to be found in English books prior to Walpole's *Letters*. At random I took up an old copy of de Joinville's and Marco Polo's books to discover what word these aforetime travellers used in their writings. I found that they " marvelled," that they found things " strange," that they " looked very earnestly."

The other eyes that Kema brings to my mind had intense fixity and fear. They were the bare, unlidded eyes of a giant turtle which was being carried from the maternal comfort of the sea by six men. Its flappers were bent back and tied to poles of wood. Thus painfully was it carried to some horrid end. Its eyes hurt me for ever. They showed no thought, nothing but fear.

The rain ceased, so we got into the canoe, a native dug-out with a sail. Four Malays were ready, three to paddle and one to steer. Now and then a breeze sprang up and we were able to sail ; but we spent five hours on the sea, going in all sixteen miles, and we missed the favour of the tide through the childishness of the crew. These men talked and smoked without ceasing. Taking up our leather coats which we had with us to cover our camp beds, they asked: " What is the price of this, and this ? " pointing to our various belongings. " Surely no country is so cold that you must wear such thick coats ! "

In Liroeng and Rurukan, and later on in mid-Celebes, I marvelled at the childlikeness of the people. With no background of history or of literature, with no culture and no spirituality, the Celeban faces the world in the debonair fashion of a smiling child. The seasons do not threaten his substance with lack of rain or lack of sunshine, he has no fears, no burdens. No tyrannical clocks tick away his life. The sun's movements are precise enough, and by those he marks his actions. " I will return when the sun is there," a man will say, pointing to the place in the sky where it will pass. The sun is his clock and his milestone. So to the Explorer's oft-repeated " How many miles more ? " when we journeyed through mid-Celebes, the leader would answer, pointing to the sky : " The sun will be there when next we stop."

A breeze sprang up, and we entered the Straits of Limbe, which lie between the island of Limbe and the extreme north-west of Celebes. The straits were full of sea craft. Canoes surrounded us, and sailing boats with small meshed nets hanging high over the bow ; for we were in waters known to the fishermen of the Moluccas and of Borneo. The fish here caught were sold to Mr. Wang, the man to whom we were making our way.

ALLAMANDA CATHARTICA.

To face page 180.

The fish shot up before us in silvery sprays. Little fish leapt into the air to avoid the onrush of the monsters of the sea. The wind rippled the surface of the water, which was also moved by the coming and going of shoals of fish, and so pulsed with a two-fold beat. We saw the form of a great black whale, and many pig fish that added to the panic. The pig fish were horrid creatures, their backs like dolphins and their heads like pigs, with greedy snouts. Fish eagles and kites and terns hunted with great swoops in the teeming spaces of these seas.

Bending over the side of our canoe we could see in the garden of the sea that the coral grew scarlet and emerald and brown. " Grew," should I say, when its formation is the work of centuries? Before roses evolved from the primal single briar, these simple creatures were nearly as complete as now we saw them. They had in their long growth taken the forms of mushrooms, of sponges and hobgoblin plants. They were, of course, endowed with life; they impressed me with their age. Our transitory land-flowers blossomed and faded through a thousand summers whilst these forms assumed their leisurely outlines. The illusion remained that this was a veritable garden, the garden of Neptune, planted for the Sirens. Blue star-fish and queer little beings striped in the fashion of zebras swam amid the coral.

Do you know the kind of impossible green that only a child, and rather a naughty child, finds in its paint box? Well, that green showed in the gardens of the sea.

We arrived after sunset, very stiff, very cramped, and wetted by the brief, sudden rains. Down to the water side ran a little Chinaman, Mr. Wang, and he waved his hand and called, "Good-bye, good-bye." "He does not want us to land: we must go back," I said disconsolately, but the Explorer went ashore. Then our future host took all care from us by leading us to his house and ordering our things to be carried up behind us.

He only knew two words in English, the words were "good-bye." This was his welcome.

We had been told that his house was very fine, but the bedroom that was offered us, and which Mr. Wang afterwards inhabited with his wife, was a passage-room leading to a sorting-room behind. Only half the floor was boarded, the other earthen half was moving with ants. It held two beds, with wooden boards in lieu of mattresses. Under the beds was a fantastic medley. There were baskets full of birds' nests to be used for soup, and a lot of bêche-de-mer, that giant black sea slug beloved of China-men; there were various condiments for cooking, and much else besides. We decided to use a corner of the verandah and merely to keep a few clothes slung along a wire through this room. A bamboo hut was built for our ablutions.

The kitchen was opposite the verandah. Mr. Wang liked nothing better than cooking, and I cooked our meals there, because our tastes differed from his. I also taught Mrs. Wang to make bread, though kneading it in the great heat was wearisome. Mrs.

Wang was a Christian from the Minahassa, much younger than her husband, and very shy. Just below the verandah in front of the house, about three yards from our chairs and table, was a narrow stream of water, where the servants washed the plates, and the labourers cleaned the masses of fish that were brought in from the straits and dried and smoked them for Chinese consumption in Menado. Geese, dogs and pigs made great clamour all day, contesting for the offal of the fish which was thrown away into the stream. The fisherman shared with Mr. Wang the profit of the sales of the fish. The Chinaman sold oyster shells for buttons, birds' nests and bêche-de-mer, but his main hope for wealth is hope deferred for four years, when he should reap the harvest of the coconut plantation.

CHAPTER XIV

HUNTING THE ANOA

"But I dare not, dare not miss,
    Cooped in houses, wind and rain;
I may never come again
This way; I must see this place,
All its beauty, face to face
Suns and moons, and tossing trees."
                                    F. NIVEN.

AT six o'clock one morning we were paddled in a long
canoe to a distant plantation that belonged to a man
of the Minahassa. Only a few labourers worked in
the plantation, which was said to be a frequent resort
of the anoa, or, as the Malays term it, the sapi-utan
—that is, the " Bull of the Jungle."

Venus, most beautiful and softly bright, had faded
into the sunrise. The waters mirrored the colours of
the sky, whilst below in the garden of the sea the
shapes and colours of the coral again stirred us to
wonder.

Anchored near Mr. Wang's plantation were many
small boats, the dwellings of some of his workmen.
On a few boards under a low thatch children are born
and bred, chickens are raised, food is prepared and
cooked, the whole life cycle of the little family is enacted.
The lack of space would seem to make it impossible
so to live. The heat below the thatch must be

intense, the stench overwhelming. One result of this way of living is that it ages its victim; women of thirty look old, whilst men of fifty are enfeebled.

There are, in the Orient, sea gypsies whose lives are passed in much the same way, save that they are entirely children of the sea and suffer sickness if they have to stay on shore. They live on fish, and their home is a canoe of fifteen feet long.

We arrived at a black volcanic beach. In the cindery soil we read the history of this part of Celebes. We could imagine its dramatic birth, in a burst of volcanic upheaval from out the sea. An old huntsman met us and told Mr. Wang that a Dutch wise man (professor of seismology), had just visited the volcano beyond us, and had left a message for Mr. Wang. The message was to warn him that the volcano must erupt soon, and might, at any hour, break into violence. In instant imagination I saw this whole point of land swept by masses of burning lava, and the sea rising up into a huge tidal wave that would sweep like a terrible wall of death through all the narrow sea. Mr. Wang only said, " No, no, it could not destroy the land this year."

After walking for almost half an hour, I was able to tell Talbot that I was getting used to the volcano, of which he had thought no more. How rapidly does the known dissolve our fears !

A boy went before us with a chopper to hack down the underwood, a rugged elder brother followed with a spear. The old huntsman came with three companions to carry the camera, the gun and the rifle.

Several fat dogs came also, the first friendly and well-fed dogs that we had seen among the natives of the Dutch Indies. Their masters were Christians. We were warned that if we wounded the sapi it would charge us, and that the men would swarm up the trees.

Only at the very end of the march did I discover that we were following a path which each man keeps cleared as he passes. As long as we were on the path I never imagined for a moment that anyone else had ever before come this way. Once, by mistake, we strayed from the path. Then and then only did I realise how dense is the jungle where no man has walked.

During five hours we sought the anoa, and we covered only about two miles an hour. We blazed our path as we went, that is, the men cut down palms to mark the trail. We had to swing over fallen trees and crawl under low-lying branches to work through long trailing rattan coils ; even the cobwebs in the trees were dense and strong enough to catch and hold us. We grew terribly exhausted. We saw tracks of sapi-utan, which the dogs were to round up so that Talbot might be able to shoot it.

The jungle here was strange. It was so dense that I saw only stems, and a tangle of leaves, and everywhere thorns. The jungle seemed more the outward form of an evil thought than a work of nature. It expressed malevolence. If " pity has a human face " then mercilessness might be made manifest as this jungle. Here grew a tree the leaves of which were poison, and one of the men wrenched me roughly away as I neared it. He said : " Had you touched a leaf, or even gone nearer to that tree, your skin would have risen up in horrible sores, you would have died in torment, tearing at the wounds." The low palms, the long stems of plants, the tree trunks, even the leaves of some of the trees and creepers were beset with thorns. Often I nearly fell, and as I threw out my hands for support, I was pierced deeply.

There were poisonous trees from which, if a leaf were broken off, a white milky substance oozed forth. This was a milk of venom ; the very ashes of the tree when burned would kill a child if mixed with his food. Near it grew another tree, the fruits of which had power to undo this evil.

Thus the plants and the palms and the trees threatened us, the animal kingdom also was full of our enemies.

There were centipedes, scorpions and snakes, and wasps with hanging nests. At night, there were harmful bats. We passed a small orange-coloured snake, and the Malay nearest it jumped back with his naked feet whilst Talbot beat it to death. Had one of us been bitten, he would have died instantly, unless the healing fruit of a certain tree was within reach to heal the hurt.

I knew that the waters of the straits were full of dangers, that the coral gives a poisonous cut, that eleven different kinds of fish have venomous stings, and that the flesh of a twelfth if eaten is fatal to man. But when I asked the youth who walked nearest to me if he feared the volcano or the snakes, or any of the creatures or plants that surrounded his life, he told me that his people fear only the "hantu," an evil spirit or ghost, that here flies at night in the form of a ball of fire. When it enters into a house or a boat it destroys the people.

I saw many lights at night on the seas and on the shore; I never saw so many anywhere else in the world. There were the stars above and phosphorescence below, and glow-worms and fire-flies.

At night the trees were festooned with luminous insects. Every leaf, stem and branch was engirdled with them : the air was gay with their shining. The stars were very clear, mirrored in the waters which broke into a second brilliance every time the oar clove the water.

The light of the "hantu" I never saw. Strange that with so many real and tangible terrors these men should fear only the immaterial magic menace of the hantu. Their tangible enemies were familiar and part of their daily lives, and many of them had their known antidotes. They had power to appal me as being strange and new, but by the children of the jungle the evil sprite alone was to be feared.

Here and there in the jungle we saw magnificent spaces where great palms grew with massive stems like pillars. No birds sang, but in such a space we heard many hornbills rising from the palms, with a great flapping of wings and strange harsh notes like the sound of a dog barking. We saw birds as large as geese, with white tails, and knew them to be

"THE BIRDS THAT EMBITTERED BUFFON!"
The Hornbill—The Cranorrhinus Cassidix.

THE BLACK APE.
Cynopithecus Nigrescens.

To face page 188.

the hornbills of Celebes, the Cranorrhinus Cassidix. They differ, though not greatly, from the other fifty varieties in the world. A deep red casque of horn rises above their eyes. They are grandly helmeted with horn of scarlet and gold, and round their eyes is a marking of bright blue. They flew in companies over us, and filled me with so many thoughts that I sat down and watched them as well as I could through the thick roofing of the trees. So these were the birds that Pliny ranked with Pegasus and with the griffons, and I was looking at them !—these the birds that embittered Buffon against Nature, therefore against God, when he pondered what he mistakenly imagined to be an injustice inflicted upon them ; he thought that their great beaks, that look so heavy and are so light, prevented their being able to obtain food to suffice them. The bird's orange bill is ridged and grooved at the base, and with it the male closes up his mate as soon as she begins to lay. He cloisters her in a hole in a tree, and cuts her off from the outside world as though he were an Eastern potentate and she his highest wife. He leaves a small opening through which he feeds her and the young with his useful beak. With it he devours snakes, first tossing them into the air, then catching and swallowing them. Strangest of all, Nature allows him to harbour and then to eject through the great bill a precious secretion which, formed like a sack, contains fruit that the bird has eaten, and this is a cornucopia that provides food for the mother hornbill.

Rain fell, but so dense was the canopy of the palms above us that we were not wetted. These gigantic palms rose a hundred feet or more on their smooth, rounded, tower-like stems. Their fan-shaped leaves, some seven feet broad, shut off the light from the earth beneath, thereby creating spaces like vast naves in the otherwise unshapely medley of vegetation.

We saw also the smaller hornbill, Rhabdotorhinus exaratus, and many baboon-like monkeys, Cynopithecus nigrescens, with fiery-coloured callosities and over-hanging brows; each was as big as a spaniel. They belonged only to Celebes, unique denizens of this group of islands so rich in creatures peculiar to itself. By the shore we saw a maleo—" maleo del pante " the men called it, and it was distinct from the megapod though of the same family. It ran by quickly, a flash of black and white and glowing pink, then was gone again.

We came once very close to the volcano and walked in an open space that circled about it for miles. Here were cinders, deep fissures and ravines, and long coarse grass with shrubs. Here also were many tamarisks. We saw some deer, but they were out of range. " Orang Mahi" (" Old man "), I said to the Chief, " How much further have we to go ? " " For another hour," he said, and when the hour was over I asked again. " Another hour," he answered. When that also had passed I repeated my question, but he did not dare answer in the same way, and said, " we have still far to go." After this last saying we walked only for half an hour and then found ourselves back on the seashore near our canoe.

These natives hunt in such a way that they have but

a slight chance of coming upon a beast; they hoped that the dogs would round up a sapi-utan and bring it within shot. Still-hunting would, however, have been difficult in this fearsome jungle, as there is almost a complete absence of streams or pits of water. The dwellers on the shore sides had to go far up the coast for fresh water. To quench his thirst one of the men with us cut some creeping tendril and drank the watery substance that trickled from it.

Before the expedition ended Talbot was groaning with fatigue. I was too proud to groan and treated him haughtily when he expressed his weariness, yet when we got back into the canoe I suffered such agonies of cramp that I surprised the crew and myself by crying violently! For nearly two days the cramp persisted at intervals. Talbot suffered for five days from a finger which he had poisoned with one of the leaves of the jungle.

A week later we tried again to find an anoa. That time we slept under a palm thatch near the volcano, and on the morrow went on another trail through sharp-edged grass which grew higher than our heads. This second time, though we only went half as far as before, we saw many traces of the anoa, but never got near to a beast.

CHAPTER XV

GOOD-BYE TO MR. WANG

"They like to do everything for themselves, to see for
themselves, and to shoot animals for themselves."
Mr. Wang musing on the English.[1]

WE stayed with Mr. Wang for ten days. He remains
in my mind as a courageous being. Born and bred in
Celebes, he could not speak Chinese, but he was a
disciple of Confucius, and often read a well-worn
Malay translation of that sage's philosophy. He had
lived in Menado, where he had made money in business
and rejoiced in a Chinese wife and nine children. He
had reached the age of forty, and was looking forward
to the enhanced regard gradually ripening to veneration
which makes old age so happy a time to the Chinese.
Through another's dishonesty he became bankrupt.
He left his family in Menado. He came to this
jungle and with six natives cleared four miles of it,
rid it of growth and undergrowth so dense that from
the waters of the straits the uncleared jungle just
below his coconut garden looked like a black wall.
When this Herculean task was performed, he planted
four thousand coconut palms in the receptive earth.

[1] Talbot had just refused to buy the head of an *Anoa depressicornis*
that had been trapped in the jungle.

"IN FRONT OF OUR VERANDAH."

Photographs by J. Talbot Clifton.

"HE FELL INTO THAT POSTURE."

To face page 193.

He built the house, then, lest he should fall sick and need to be nursed, he took a Minahassa girl as secondary wife. The marriages of the Chinese in the Dutch Indies had not been registered till a very few years ago. The official mode of addressing them on envelopes had been " Wang," or whatever surname the recipient had, and below was written " Chinaman." One day a sturdy son of China replied to a Dutch official, " Mynheer—Dutchman." This caused a tremendous commotion among the officials, but the mode of address to Celestials was altered henceforth.

The lazy, lifeless Lutheran girl did not greatly add to Mr. Wang's comfort. When making bread, she would not knead the dough enough to make it rise.

When Wang laughed, which he often did, he stamped on the ground and lifted up his feet and waved above his head his thin fingers with their long nails. He had pleasing attitudes, almost heraldic. Look at him in the picture holding up a healing leaf wherewith to protect or heal me from the poison tree under which I am sitting. He fell into that posture with great simplicity, but it conjured up for me a whole people, a civilisation, and a worship derived from remote antiquity and translated from China to Celebes.

He could now let his nails grow long, for he had one hundred and fifty-nine men to work for him, and the responsibility of over three hundred people, counting the women and children. He was making over a thousand pounds a year at the time we were with him by his sales of mother-of-pearl and the gastronomical merchandise that I before referred to. He did not pay much money to the labourers, but rewarded them by letting them have allotments on the ground which he had cleared. He bought rice seed and grew a crop which he exchanged against the edible nests of a species of swift and against bêche-de-mer. Four years must pass before his coconut trees would be mature enough to yield their harvest. Then he will summon a K.P.M. steamer and load her with his merchandise. Often I saw his eyes resting on the perfect harbour below his wooden house, and I knew he could, in imagination, hear the crews lowering the copra bags into the hold.

After we left him we never heard how Mr. Wang fared, but we wish him well.

CHAPTER XVI

MENADO TO POSSO

"There are . . . things which are too wonderful for me . . .
The way of a ship in the midst of the sea."
Proverbs.

On the 14th June we sailed from Menado for Posso
on the *Van Waerwijck*, commanded by Captain Götz.
She was over 3,000 tons, and was bound for the north-
eastern ports. Amongst these ports was Gorontalo,
an important trading town, also Posso, a small military
station whither we were destined. Talbot surmised
that Posso would be a good starting place for a journey
right through the centre of Celebes to the south. We
had been told that in this country he would be able
to shoot a bos anoa. We had no precise route mapped
out, because the Explorer always lets our journeys
expand and grow around us as we go.

In the first class we were a mixed company, some of
the passengers being from Holland, notably Mynheer
Brand, a director of the K.P.M. Steamship Company,
and Mevrouw Brand, charming people newly out from
Amsterdam. A German trader there was, spectacled,
and in his hand always a little bag ; a rich Arab also,
who wore European clothes, and a fez that he kept
on and shoes that he often cast off. We had, too,

the company of a Japanese with a troubled brow and no languages.   Amongst the officers were some Austrians, because the K.P.M. could not get young Dutchmen to serve in these Indies as merchant seamen. The Company would not employ Germans, because they always wish to remain on in the Company, whereas some fifty young Austrians had arrived in these Indies from the Imperial Navy; they had contracted for five years' service, by which time the directors hoped to have some volunteers from Holland.

In the fourth class were wonderful women from the northern part of Celebes with clothes of red and blue, the bodices of which looked like Union Jacks.   In the steerage were men employed by the K.P.M. to go on shore for the coconut husks and other goods sent from the Bay of Tomini, where the people, like those of the north-west coast, are too rich and too lazy to bring out their own merchandise.   There are no piers.   The coolies have to wade through the shallow sea a long way to the waiting boats.   The coolies and passengers, other than first class, numbered over a thousand; a pleasing assembly they made with their sleeping mats and washing pots.   The coolies were Mahommedans who came from near Macassar, Bugis by race and language, a hardy lot of men.   In charge of them was an overseer, tough both of muscle and of will.

At Gorontalo so many coolies and other dark passengers wished to disembark that the gangway was full of them.   The steps became slippery and some people fell into the sea.

THE HOME OF THE SEA GYPSY.

Photograph by J. Talbot Clifton.

K.P.M. STEAMER THE "VAN RIEMSDYK."

To face page 196.

One was an old man. He hung on the bottom rung of the gangway, with his body in the sea. He was too weak to get up, but no one seemed to trouble at all about him. I suppose that these Mahommedans thought that if it was God's will he would be able to get out of the sea again, which he did. A woman who had a long box made of dried palm strapped down her back also fell into the water. Some men pulled her out and threw her head first into a canoe that was waiting to take passengers ashore.

They also threw from the deck into the same canoe chickens tied together, boxes, pans and matting. You can, perhaps, imagine the clamour.

During the whole of our journey we admired beyond measure the Steamship Company, called the Koninklijke Paketvaart Maatschappij, which for many years has carried on the trade of the Dutch East Indies. A hundred ships of 3,000 tons, and less, form its fleet. It has no rivals and yet its charges for passenger service and for carriage of cargo are most just.

These vessels are usually built with the first class passenger accommodation in the centre, whilst fore and aft under the holds are the quarters of the steerage passengers. The boat decks carry many well-built barges capable of holding several tons. On entering a port the motor launch and the barges are lowered into the water with a precision and rapidity worthy of a British man-of-war. The cabins on the ships are very comfortable, especially those on the boat deck. We were often given a cabin similar to the Captain's, with a small deck to ourselves and a private bathroom.

For this luxury we had nothing extra to pay. We were deeply indebted to the Company for their kindness in reserving for us these charming cabins. The dining rooms are usually brightly decorated with blue and white pictorial tiles. The cooking is like that of Holland, and much better than in any of the hotels in the East. The food may seem heavy for these hot countries, fat pork, sausages, and cabbage cooked in butter and oil; but in the Tropics very nourishing food is needed, and the poor quality of the meat has to be made good by using these fatty substances. On land the Dutch live otherwise, for their chief food is rice, which they eke out with a little meat and many condiments. They have eggs, tinned food, and they make their own bread.

If we wished to use the ship's motor launch to go ashore, it was always at our disposal; or sometimes the Captain would propose our accompanying him whilst he went out to dynamite fish for the evening meal. Once when, later on our travel, we found we could make no connection along the sea route we had wished to follow down the east coast, this wonderful Company actually kept a steamer waiting for two days, by which means we were enabled to carry out our plan. These favours were all freely given, as also hospitality in the ports, where often the Captain, who always spoke English, would entertain us for a day or two on the ship rather than let us go straight to the Rest House or the hotel.

We anchored at a place called Oena-Oena, which means " the Place to Behold." It is an island; in its centre is a volcano. Oena-Oena was lively ; it had moreover a rich landowner. Some years before a Bugis man had lived on this island, as also did many Malays, and each man grew his own palms. Suddenly the volcano in their midst burst into flames, and lava streamed down one side of the island. The people rushed to their boats, even Kismet was forgotten as the earth quaked and the mountain threatened them with death. The Bugis went down to the shore carrying much money. He called out to one and another, "Will you sell me your coconut trees ? " For about twopence each he bought the trees that were worth ten pounds, paying the money into the shaking hands of the Malays. They paddled away, mocking at him perhaps. He remained at Oena-Oena. The volcano ceased putting forth flames and lava, and presently the Malays came back. As though they had forgotten their fear, they returned to their plantations. The Bugis came to them and said : " You may work here, but as my servants, and no longer as owners, for you have sold all to me." They did not kill him, but they often robbed him. Therefore, although the rich volcanic soil produced excellent palms, he did not make a vast fortune.

To me he is a perfect example of Napoleon's axiom, that the main difference between one man and another, and the fate of one man and another, arises from the fact that one man will seize his opportunities whilst another does not do so.

CHAPTER XVII

GRISELDA

"I love you still till death and faithfully."

CHAUCER.

FROM one of the ports, we sailed into many, there came aboard the steamer a tragic Griselda of to-day, a patient Griselda as sorely tried as she of the story. She was a pretty, fair-haired Dutch woman, with a boy of about eight years, but she was ill and terribly pale. She came on board as we went east, but she would have to repass this port on the ship's return to Menado. There our sorrowful lady would disembark and change ships for Macassar and Batavia on her way to Holland.

She had not waited to join the steamer on its return, because she knew that this was the moment when she must free herself from a horrible slavery. If she waited, her resolve might fail her. Even now, so thought the ship's officer who told me her story, she might perhaps abandon her flight to Europe and disembark when the ship returned to this port.

She had met and married in Holland a Comptroller of good family and had come to Celebes with him. Her wedded life, at its happiest, must have been sombre. She probably left her verandah for only half an hour in the evening; she almost certainly did not ride, nor did she entertain the rare passing stranger, for, though she would have welcomed any one from Holland as she would have welcomed flaming tulips or homely delftware, yet her husband said : " My small salary must all be saved for our return to Holland."

A frail baby boy was born. Mevrouw wilted and grew paler. The monotony of the Tropics weighed upon her; she wearied of the unchanging seasons, the unchanging fashions of the native women, the stagnation of the East. The Comptroller, seeing her listlessness, was at first worried, then angry. " The men are wise who live with the women of the country," he said. Soon after he found a young Christian of the Minahassa and took her into the house as sewing maid and as his mistress. A little later some money was left to him, enough to retire on and to return to Holland, but though he now left the Government service, he would not leave the country. His family had had a long past in these colonies. It is likely that he had the blood of the Indies in his veins. Now the country claimed him as its own.

He moved out of the Government house. His wife and his mistress followed him. Their new home grew dirty. Mevrouw tried wearily for a little while to remain European, but the heat, and the ants, and the natives undid her. She loved her husband too much to leave him, so she shared him with the native woman. Her small boy grew taller and paler. Her husband became untidy and more and more lazy, smoking endless cigarettes to the sound of the gramophone. He remained unshaven, and at the evening meal he never now donned a stiff white suit and collar, but lounged in pyjamas, which were not as freshly starched or as often changed as they used to be. One day Mevrouw and her husband had a bitter quarrel. A native, who often came to the house, taught their boy wantonly to torture a cat. The woman saw suddenly in a blinding light the whole horror of the position. She had made excuses for her husband, had blinded herself to the hideousness of her lot, and with love and a wild philosophy had kept up illusion in her mind. " Man needed a dual life, one woman to minister to his body and another to his mind." So she had tried to think. " This return to nature and simplicity was not evil but good." Her infatuation for her husband doped her reason. The fiction crumpled up before the brutal fact that the child was being corrupted. For him the return to wholesome cleanly Holland was vital ; for her, geographical details were unimportant, for when the heart is broken nothing matters. She told the ex-Comptroller she would await him in Holland, that he could follow her, that he might bring his native woman if he so desired, but that the boy must return to the land of his race. She looked for the last time on the house of growing dirt and disorder, on the woman already big with child by her husband, on the monkey chained to the tree, on the screaming parrot and the maltreated cat. Then, with her boy, she boarded the steamer.

CHAPTER XVIII

POSSO

"Two women shall be grinding at a mill ;
The one shall be taken and the other left."
Gospels.

BEFORE we reached Posso, the Explorer suffered
terrible and increasing pain for three days.   Feverish
and nearly delirious, he lay on his camp bed on deck
hardly able to walk, whilst a swelling on his groin grew
bigger and bigger.

In the whole of Celebes there are only three or four
Dutch doctors.   By good fortune a military surgeon
was stationed at Posso.   When we anchored there,
Dr. Van der Veer came on board and diagnosed the
trouble as being a phlegmon, and he said that Talbot
must come ashore and wait eleven days[1] for the
coming of the next steamer.   Rain was falling in
torrents, but Mr. Brand, in charity, accompanied us on
shore.   The phlegmon—which was not an abscess,
though it looked, as an Oriental would say, like the
grandfather of abscesses—was caused by bacilli.   It had
to be lanced, and the resultant wound was several inches
long.   The Explorer was only ready to travel when
the ship *Van Rees*, commanded by Captain Blomhert,
called at Posso nine days later.   The customs of
the colonials in these Indies were entirely right for a
pleasant regaining of health, for Talbot could, with

[1] She came in two days early.

perfect regard to his hostess, lie in her verandah in his pyjamas, his slippered feet pointing to the sea.

Posso was the ultimate place in this region to be taken over by the Dutch; that roads might be made, that the country might be, as it were, combed out. Posso was populated chiefly by Arabs, whose head and representative was a Hadji.

One mile of coral road ran through Posso; beyond that came the jungle. A line of pretty bungalows shaded by coconut palms faced the sea; behind them lay the Mission House, the shop, the school, and the Comptroller's house, whilst beyond these were the barracks and the hospital. Squads of convicts cleaned the town and acted as gardeners and roadmakers. There were also sixty soldiers and three Dutch officers, Doctor Van der Veer being one of them.

In the barracks were three Dutch sergeants. One of them had a Javanese wife, the second had a mistress from Menado, whilst the third had till lately enjoyed a native mistress, but he had been obliged to leave her behind in his former station, because a new rule had been made forbidding Christian soldiers to keep a mistress in barracks. This law did not sunder lovers long united. Hence the good fortune of the second sergeant.

Mevrouw Van der Veer was a wonderful little lady. The apathy of the East had not absorbed her. She and her husband always dressed themselves in European clothes. She had forgotten the French and English that she had learnt, and as the Dutch will not talk to other Europeans in Malay, it was sometimes difficult for us to exchange ideas; but there was a flow of sympathy between us, and I was able to help her with her household affairs, besides cooking for my own invalid. We found we were able to buy fowls, and sometimes fish, once even a small pig, so that we got fresh meat. I never ceased marvelling at the fact that in the Dutch Indies, which are carefully and ably governed by so pastoral a people as the Dutch, it is impossible to have fresh milk. Millions of pounds worth of condensed milk is imported each year, and the officials, whenever questioned, always declare it to be impossible to keep milch cows. The convicts or the natives doing compulsory labour might well cut and bring in fodder for cows, but this is never done.

Strange figures came down the white coral road which for ten days I looked out upon from dawn to dusk. The Rajah of Posso would pass looking comely in khaki, with a gold and purple head coif and a sarong folded round his waist, followed by almost nude men with scarves of red. Once a Dutch woman, Mevrouw Adrian, from an outlying mission eighteen miles away, walked in to see the doctor because she was ill. She did not seem to be exhausted.

A child, whom a mad dog had bitten, came down among the palms one morning. He was given an injection by the doctor, and was sent off with a soldier to the port of Dongalla, separated by some four days' hard walking. There they would get a steamer for Batavia, where the child would be given the Pasteur treatment. A native of Posso went by also, with a terribly poisoned leg. He had just refused to have it cut off by the doctor. " Not even if you allow me to take it away afterwards," he answered. He went to his village, himself cut out the abscess, and died the same day. Some Arabs, too, went by, seeking the hospital ; two ill-starred beings, and a third whom fate was about to favour. One of them, a man of forty, had a diseased leg. Dr. Van der Veer said : " You must let me cut it off," but the Arab replied : " This would maim me not only on earth, but also in Paradise. I must ask my father's will. I will send my friend to plead with him ; it is but a three days' journey." The father was away, so the Captain of the Arabs at Posso signed a scroll allowing that the limb be severed. By this time death had claimed the man. The second Arab had an abscess on the liver. He was operated upon, but died. To the great rage of his countrymen, he now haunts the hospital. Strangely enough, the third man, who had walked with the other two on the white road, also had an abscess on his liver, although he did not know that this was so. He said to a friend : " I will not go to the white doctor. Plunge a knife into me here, I feel that it would ease my pain." Without horror or squeamishness, the friend did as he was asked, and out flowed all the evil humours. So the man lived, according to Allah's will, whereas the other, tended with chloroform and having availed himself of skilled modern surgery, died, and is a ghost.

So passed the days whilst I watched the road and tended Talbot. Then the ship arrived and we sailed away.

CHAPTER XIX

SONGS AND STORIES OF NORTH-EAST CELEBES

"'Once . . . once upon a time . . .'
Like a dream you dream in the night,
Fairies and gnomes stole out
In the leaf-green light."
WALTER DE LA MARE.

WALLACE divided the people of the Malay Archipelago into two well-defined races : the Papuans of New Guinea and some neighbouring isles, and the Malays. Of the Papuans we saw nothing. The true Malay race he breaks up in four main parts, with a fringe of semi-civilized tribes and of savages. These four branches are : The Malays proper, who people the Malay Peninsula and the coasts of Borneo and Sumatra ; the Javanese of Java, and of parts of Sumatra, Bali and Lombok ; the Bugis, who inhabit many parts of Celebes and Sumbaya ; and the Tagalas, people of the Philippine Isles.

We were told that in Celebes there are thirty-three languages, and after crossing the island on foot, as will be related, I well believed this. The extracts of the north-eastern literature, which I will give, I obtained from Mrs. Adriani in exchange for a present to the Mission. Dr. Adriani we did not see, but he had been in these parts for nearly forty years garnering a vast harvest of the vocal traditions, songs, romances, tales, proverbs and fairy tales. He had classified them into thirteen varieties of literature.

I asked for a human story, and obtained the mythic one that follows. Mevrouw Adriani was sorry that I asked for a human one. She said the fairy tales were beautiful, the leading parts being taken by animals. The Toraja people have pondered the habits and actions of animals, and in these tales each beast speaks according to its nature. Mevrouw Adriani also said: " The Barée people ever seek the cause of events in the supernatural, an ordinary common report of daily life has, for them, no romantic worth." The teller of tales is preoccupied with the cause of things, tracing every-day happenings back to the invisible and supernatural world. " As for music," she continued, " we have not been able to write down the many songs the Toraja sing in notes—the intervals are too small. This is a great pity. We like their songs and melodies very much, but are not able to reproduce them in any writing."

I shall re-tell you a story of the Pajapi tribe, recited in the hamlets after the rice is plucked, stalk by stalk. It is gathered into large golden bunches. I have seen such bunches tied on to poles and borne on the shoulders of two men. Whilst the rice is growing such tales cannot be told, for they are the histories of ancestors, and the dead might avenge them-selves did they hear the mention of their names. They would destroy the rice crops if they heard their adventures uttered lightly. Here then is my story :

Generations and generations ago there lived in this country a brother and a sister, ancestors of the Pajapi tribe. The wealth of the brother was a dog clever in hunting wild pig. The wealth of the sister was a fish eagle that planed over the waves and caught fish for its mistress, therewith filling a basket. The brother watched his sister and saw how she lay in the hut at ease whilst the eagle hunted in the sea. He also marked how short a time she took to prepare the fish for food, whilst he had to go far into the jungle with his dog to hunt. After his dog had rounded up a pig and he had slain it, he had to cut it up and bring it back; his labour was in all ways greater than hers. This vexed and angered him, and he said : " My sister gets her food without toil. If I had the sea eagle I should no more be troubled going out hunting with my dog." Next day he went to her and said : " Sister, lend me your eagle, I wish for fish, for to-night there is feasting, and the meat I have is not enough. Lend me your eagle." She gave her bird into his care, and he went to the seashore. He broke its wings in his rage and jealousy. In the evening he took the eagle back to his sister, saying : " Here is the fish eagle, but its wings are broken. I did not break them." She, looking on the drooping bird, was long silent. She did not believe her brother's words. Slowly anger burnt within her, and she rose up and said to him : " I will live here no longer, I will go to the other side of the sea, I and my slaves will go there. If you did not break the eagle's wings, then may my race cease, and my followers be barren. We will die on the yonder side of the sea, in solitude and silence, where no children are. With dry heart and weeping eyes we shall perish, leaving none behind us. If you have lied to me, if you did break the wings of my eagle, may you not be fertile ! On you and on your people be the death of your race ! " She went to the seashore, she and her subjects, and they hewed down trees and made canoes. When all was ready they embarked. They rowed to the other side of the sea and stayed there. They bore children, they increased, and flourished, and her race is our race, the people of the Pajapi. But her brother and his people saw their generation fade away, for all were barren. Some of them, it is said, became sea pirates, but the race died out because of the lie that the brother spoke to his sister after he had broken the wings of the fish eagle.

This story surprises me because of its persistent stress on the untruth of the brother, and I wonder at so great an importance being laid on truthfulness in this, the East. I wrote asking which are the moral qualities that are most dear to the Toraja people, and I was told :

1. Liberality, that is, giving much to others.
2. Courage.
3. Eloquence.
4. Fertility that the tribe may increase in numbers.

Many tales are told in mockery of the tribe of Ondae, a mountain people that rarely visits the seashore.

Here are two such stories :

" A dweller on the mountain once went far from his village to the sea. When he saw the little waves beating on the shore, he laughed, saying :

" Here is a playmate for my children," and he scooped a wavelet into a hollow bamboo and took it back to his home, uphill and down hill along a hard way. But when he poured it out into a coconut shell, it lay listless and dull. Sick at heart, the man said : " the water dies with longing for its mother, it will not play or dance ; I must take it back to its mother."

For seven nights he travelled and, coming to the shore, he poured the water back into the sea. It was broken up by a wave and danced and glistened. " How wise I was," he said, " I knew that it was longing for its mother ! "

The second story tells of a little company of Ondae people who wished to take their coconuts over the sea in a canoe. They, being of the tribe of Ondae, forgot to put afloat the little vessel, so that, try as they might, they did not move from the spot. At last one of them cried out, saying : " We are yet ashore, we are not afloat." Upon that they pushed their boat out on to the waters, yet still they went no further, but one half of the company faced the stern and the other half faced the prow, and therefore, though they pulled fiercely, they hardly moved. Then the cleverest amongst them said : " The canoe is too heavily charged, let half the men stand up, holding the coconuts on their shoulders, that the weight may be lessened." Then one half of the company patiently held the nuts whilst the other half rowed, and the canoe glided forward. " You see," said the wise counsellor, " I was right, the weight was too great."

Dr. Adriani further wrote to me that the Toraja people has no tabulated laws, for as writing is unknown, there is only a vocal tradition whereby certain classical verdicts are fixed, and these are immortalized in metaphors which all men understand and which immediately conjure up before them certain offences and the consequent punishment. Capital punishment or a fine are the only two punishments the Toraja people inflicts. I shall now use Mrs. Adriani's own words :

" For instance, when a man takes a second wife without the consent of his wife, he has to pay a fine, which is called : ' *the gift which tears off the nails.*' Every Toraja understands that this means the paying of one or two buffaloes, the consequence of which is the tearing (or cutting) off of the wife's nails. In case this fine is not paid by the husband, the wife has the right to scratch her husband in his face.

" It is not advisable to marry a girl whose elder sister is not yet married. A man who wants to do this has to pay a fine which is called ' *for the passing by*,' e.g. the passing of the elder sister.

" If an old man wants to marry a young girl, it may be the girl is being teased by her friends because of her old husband. So the old man gives one or two buffaloes to his young wife ; this fine is called the *young maker*.

"When the young wife has received this gift, there is an end of teasing."

Adultery, high-treason and witchcraft were, by the Toraja chieftains, punished with death.

Dr. Adriani sent me also a love poem of which I transcribe the Barée original with a translation. These poems always consist of four lines, of which the third and fourth lines should contain as far as possible the same words as the first and second lines. The last four lines of this poem will show that the words are repeated with but a slight difference. The words often have to be substituted by synonyms so as to maintain the rhyme, and the rhyme is determined by the vowels of the last two syllables, regardless of the consonants: a, i, ali, o, u, oku, wuja—dunja—reme—lele—ja-u-jaku. An English example of this rhyme would be Mona, which would rhyme with Lola, and "umbra" with "junta." An English analogy may be found in some of our English Nursery Rhymes: "Tucker," "Supper," "Butter."

LOVE POEM

Rontapi wana kuliu sima'i
Mampomawo i Mojoku Ntimali
Rontapi wana kuliu silo'u
Pampomawoku i Mojoku-joku.

Lindja ngkuma'i mamporara wuja
Madonqe doro ri lipu ntadu nja
Lindja ngkuma'i mamporara reme
Madonqe doro ri lipu ntolele.

Mangura sa siko jau
Djamo mawongko rajaku
A'i, sike mangura sa,
Dja kupokawongko ndaja.

T sema mowambo lo'e ?
Ewa toroli kudonge !
Sema kudonqe mowamba ?
Ewa djaledja mandjaja !

Mowamba ane da kami
Wore wana rua ntapi
Ane kami da mowamba
Rua ntapi wore wana.

Translation :

Thro' two woods I have walked a long way to be here
For desire of the girl with a bracelet on each arm
Through two vast woods I have walked to get here
For desire of the girl wearing white shell bracelets.

I have come here in the moonshine
For I heard the stir of the feast in the village of the chief
I have come here in the sunshine
For I heard the stir of the feast in the village of the headman.

You look so lovely
I have pleasure in seeing you,
Little one you look so lovely
You please me indeed.

Who else can sing as you do,
It seems to me that I hear a bird,
Who is it I hear singing
Like a host of little birds ?

> If we two sing together
> Our song will resound thro' two woods,
> If we two together sing
> Through two woods our song will resound.

I have also some samples of the proverb poems of which the people are very fond. I will again write the original wording, as it is interesting to see how few words are used to convey the meaning, and also I will give the translation and transcription into ideas familiar to us.

> Mawuti ntja i Togou
> Mampobantjoe kajuka!
> Ara nusaja to o'ku ?
> I Rea nto Mata Ngoju.

TRANSLATION :

> He is wrong in what he has done
> He who swings there on the coconut branch !
> Do you not know my name ?
> I am the daughter of the King of the Winds.

Which being interpreted means merely :

" He may expect tit for tat." He sits like a he dove on a high palm, he vaunts and extols himself, he thinks I am a feeble girl, but let him beware for I am the daughter of the King of the Winds, and wind can be the cause of much trouble to birds.

> Wawu ngkupowawu—wawu
> Mosompo lai ampaku
> Kuloe—Loeka labu
> Koerata, roo ndasaju.

TRANSLATION:

The wild pig that I thought was mine,
The which was caught by my trap,
And near which I had hung my hunting things,
Was cut up with this my knife and taken away.

Which means that a man may hurt himself by his own lack of shrewdness. This hunter caught a boar, and hung his knife near the trap to mark the animal as his belonging. He then went to his village for help, and returned to find that another had used his knife to cut up and to steal away the creature that he had trapped.

CHAPTER XX

TERNATE, MACASSAR AND PANTJANA

"There is no human felicity but in excitement."
SIR HENRY MORGAN, Buccaneer.

DURING long hours of illness spent on the verandah in Posso, Talbot had been making a great plan. We would sail down the east coast of Celebes, and were determined to walk and ride from some part of the Gulf of Boni straight up to Posso again. Talbot reckoned this would be almost 100 miles.[1] When we boarded the s.s. *Van Rees*, Captain Blomhert told us that he would not be sailing according to his itinerary, but he must go to Ternate in Halmahera to pick up some twenty people who had been left there owing to two steamers having failed to call, as they had been damaged on rocks in these uncharted seas. Captain Blomhert pointed to a reef that was visible now because the tide was low, and he laughed, saying "A Chinaman who sails here told me that this part is clear of rocks, and I have to sail by the tales of such people." We saw that our plans, always very fluid, must now be changed, and that we must perforce return by the west coast of Macassar, and from

[1] As will be seen later, we underestimated the distance from south to north Celebes.

Macassar sail to Boni, instead of reaching Boni by the eastern coast.

Ternate is unforgettable. Its merchandise is fantastic; it no longer produces the spices which made it famous in the time of Drake, but now its wealth is its fruits, orchids and red parrots, green and white parrots, birds of paradise and big blue pigeons. It— with some other smaller isles—was the " Moluccas " of ancient adventure, the home of the clove and the nutmeg. The Netherlanders succeeded the Portuguese as conquerors of these isles, and with the Rajahs they decreed that all the spices were to be destroyed so that the Dutch might have a limited and easily managed production on their hands. The wealth and power of the Sultans of Ternate, formerly so great, gradually lessened under the alien rule till, shortly before our visit to Ternate, the last Sultan was exiled to Java. He was sent away with his son, but of his twenty-five women none followed him.

I think that a native ruler under the Dutch has less chance of survival than one under the British flag. When we find native chiefs unruly we depose them, and replace them by a near kinsman ; but rajahs under the Dutch have to be very submissive and very economical; few survive. Often these native princes were aggressive and cruel and had no real culture, so that their loss to the world is not great. Alas ! that their eclipse darkened the feelings of loyalty and of national individuality that they inspired in their people. This loss is great.

We walked in the old town, formerly called Sultan

Town, where the houses were all Portuguese fifteenth century buildings. They were constructed of thick stone and mortar, with fine polished wooden pillars and a handsome thatch. Each one had a porch, like a lych-gate, made of this thick wall, with seats on either side and a thatch above. The old fort and cannons and gate were stately.

From Posso to Macassar we journeyed for eleven quiet days. The all-embracing sun, the azure skies and seas were cordial to us. The easy movement of the ship fulfilled that demand, that lust, of our Western minds to be for ever fluxive. We anchored at Balikh Papan in Borneo, but we were not allowed to see the oil company buildings or the pipe which carries oil for many miles from the jungle. A Dutch company had pioneered the business, had lost on it and sold it to Americans, who in turn sold it to the present company from Holland, which had good expectations of big profits.

On the 12th of July we landed at Macassar and went to the Orangi Hotel which I had before found unbearable; but either its management or else my temper had improved for I was now able to endure it. Probably my residence in Liroeng and on the coconut plantation had caused me to lose my niceness in regard to cleanliness and to palatable food. Several Dutch women lived in the hotel rather than have homes of their own. They lived most innocent, most horrible lives. The hotel was built round an earthen quadrangle, wherein grew some palms and trees, and bordering this square was a passage common to us all.

The hotel bedrooms gave on to square wooden partitions that faced the corridor. In these loose boxes the women sat, each in her own, whilst the children played, quarrelled and cried up and down the passage. The children never went out into the lovely open spaces near the great avenues of Macassar. (Down before the mighty sun the trees there threw the blackest shadows I ever saw, and the chameleons chirped their unending delight.) The women became so lazy that they would not go even to the public dining-room, though there they would have seen fresh faces and have heard other cats mewing—for the dining-room had most insistent cats. They sat in rocking chairs attired in native dress, listlessly sewing, talking sometimes to a native maid, or merely looking in front of them. Perhaps they were eating their hearts out for Holland.

I was anxious to delay our expedition across Celebes as long as possible, because Talbot had hardly recovered from his afflicted leg. A Dutch sergeant who had once taken some soldiers into the interior gave me an account of his journey which was not at all encouraging. He and others said that the density of the jungle, the height of the ascents, the leeches and the lack of all accommodation, bridges or paths, made any adventuring into the interior a feat of much difficulty. Of course the Explorer was quite unconcerned, and explained to me that the Dutch would consider it a trial to ascend any kind of hill owing to the flatness of their own country, whilst we in Scotland would climb high ones each day without trouble. In the meantime

RIVER SIDE. MACASSAR

Violet Clifton

BY THE ROADSIDE MACASSAR.

To face page 220.

it was arranged by the amiable Resident of Macassar that we should receive an invitation to spend a few days with the Queen of the Bugis, some fifty miles from Macassar.

We journeyed for two days. Solely remarkable were the sudden heights that rose in sharp ridges, masses of limestone overhung with verdure. They were shaped fantastically, some like ramparts, some like thrones, whilst others were formed like columns and buttresses, or rose in sharp peaks.

On the morning of the second day's journey from Macassar we reached the village of Pantjana, and after a little delay were received by the Datoe, the Queen of the Bugis, a lady over sixty years of age. She lived in a European-looking villa furnished in paltry style. She had expected us the previous night. As she did not know that a recalcitrant Chinaman was the cause of our lack of precision, she was inclined to be haughty and displeased with us. I weaned her from fretfulness by presenting her with a Victorian pound piece to wear on a chain, and interested her by telling her about Queen Victoria, leaving her more than ever persuaded that puissant government lies only in the hands of queens.

She had perfectly black hair, her eyes were dark and shining. She wore a purple sarong and a white jacket, and a medal which the Queen of the Netherlands had sent her, for she and in the past her mother had rendered services to the Dutch Government. Sometimes she wore masses of gold and jewels. " Her capital is on her bosom " the Comptroller said to us.

She had never learnt the Malay tongue and spoke only the Bugis language, so she was completely in the power of her evil-looking interpreter, who kept from her everything which he did not wish her to know. She had an engraving of Rembrandt's " Lesson in Anatomy," and I wondered exceedingly what the strange picture conveyed to her mind, but I could not ask. At last we bade her good-bye, and were escorted to a long bamboo house built on piles—dirty but pleasing, for it was spacious and airy and queer—the kind of house a hundred Bugis could have lived in. Many youths from the Datoe's house went with us—courtiers, I suppose—gorgeous in gay sarongs and velvet caps and with pencils stuck in the pockets of their white jackets. They wished to stand about and stare at us, but the Explorer would have none of this and set them to useful tasks such as providing us with water, of which there was none in the house.

In the evening of the next day we drove to Liso, where is the hunting box of the royal lady. There was no oil and no candles, so we bathed and ate in darkness. We slept on the verandah with a guard of chiefs around us. At four o'clock in the morning an old man chanted forth praises to Allah. " Prayer is better than sleep." This was his cry, sent up at sunrise; then for an hour and a half the chiefs chanted. At six we rose and I saw how beautiful Liso is. We beheld mountains, long seemly houses, and the hunting party all ready to start, the men being mounted on ponies and carrying long spears. We walked almost two miles through fields of tobacco plants and arrived at a valley into which the deer were to be driven. Talbot was to shoot some, and others the riders were to spear. I quite dreaded a terrible killing, but the result of four hours of waiting in the valley whilst the beaters searched the hills was only two deer, one of which Talbot shot just as it was breaking back to the jungle. The second beast was speared by the hunters.

We breakfasted, and gave the men a present, as their fatigue was great after circling the hills for us. They were very loath to take anything, saying that it was not their custom so to do. We also gave them some venison, taking some ourselves. Then a man came with a sore on his foot, which I washed and bandaged. We left with great amity on all sides and drove back.

Soon afterwards we returned to Macassar to make ready for the hundred-and-eighty mile walk through [1] Celebes. We were to pack our luggage into bundles weighing forty pounds each, because men would have to carry all that we took, and forty pounds is about the accepted weight in Celebes, as eighty pounds is—or was—in Central Africa.

We bade the wilful lady of the Bugis farewell and departed, wondering at the vigour of this race of the Celebes people.

[1] So we then, mistakenly, reckoned it.

CHAPTER XXI

GULF OF BONI

*" Blessed is he who has been able to win knowledge of
the causes of things and has cast beneath his feet all fear."*
Georgics—VIRGIL.

WE sailed from Macassar to the Salayer group of
islands, which is not notable. The only white man on
Salayer, a Netherlands' Comptroller, came on board
and warned us urgently against our proposed journey.
He had been as far as a place called Leboni on the route
which we decided upon, three days' march from the
base. He said that the journey was fearful and
horrible, there being no path, and the ascent very
painful.

Leaving the Salayer isles we headed north again for
the Gulf of Boni, which lies between the two southern
horns of Celebes, and in this gulf passed an island with
a quantity of magnesia in its soil. This journey was
enthralling. No longer, as in the north, did we see
a listless people fattening on the produce of their coconuts, too indolent to sail up with merchandise to the
steamer. Here was a virile race of Bugis people
sailing about in great wooden ships like Noah's arks,
excitable and keen, storming our ship as though
engaged in battle rather than in commerce, each boat

Violet Clifton.

"STORMING OUR SHIP."

To face page 224.

barging into the other, striving to obtain a favoured place near the crew and the hold. The men leapt into the sea or swarmed the stays. The cargo was varied and picturesque. Here were bundles of rattan from the jungle for Europeans to turn into garden chairs and tables and gum from the forest trees for Europeans to refine into resin ; here were bags of rice, maize and tobacco ; all the raw material piled on board for European use, distribution and manufacture. Here was the work of the hand, there the work of the brain ; here muscle and man, there machinery and man ; here supply and there demand ; here the fountain, there the wrought cup. Long ere this I had felt in India and Burma, and later again in Arabia, that in the East man looks inward, and in the West man looks outward, one the introspective, the other the exteriorized vision. The Eastern sage, wrapped in abstract thought, gazes at his navel and obtains self knowledge and beatitude ; the Western sage gazes at the planets, at plants, at animalcules, and lays the forces of Nature under the empire of his discovery.

The scenery brought reminiscences of Scotland's hills spread along the coast, some bare and some tree clad. Then the mind would be whirled back to the East by wonderful canoes, fifty feet long and bound together in threes, laden with merchandise, whilst on our ship, the *Swaedercroon*, the fathoms' depths of this splendid sea were chanted in a liturgical cadence by the man who swung the plummet.

We cruised past Paloppo, which was our port of disembarkation, on as far as Malili that we might see that port.   We disembarked at Paloppo on the ship's return journey.   At Port Malili we admired the noble width of the Gulf of Boni, embracing sixty miles of water.   There, in thunder and rain, came on a strange cargo.   Employed by Chinese merchants to gather resin in the jungle, and now returning to Paloppo, was a number of Toraja men and women, tribal people of a distinctive type.   They are divided into various classes and tongues, and occupy a large part of Eastern and Northern Celebes.   The men were long haired and covered with a hideous brown cloth wound round them.   The women, naked to the waist, had what appeared to be sackcloth hanging from their hips, but it was raiment made from the bark of trees. These labourers were thin and dirty, and suffered from a skin disease.   I was told that, in spite of fever and skin disease, the women walk thirty miles or more in the jungle, carrying forty pounds of resin.   These people are Pagans.   They are good to the aged.

They lay on the boards of the deck among the cattle, which were also part of the cargo.

Puppies would have chosen a more comfortable place.   The excrement of the cows, the passing and repassing of the busy crew—none of these things seemed to trouble the women, though two of them vomited after having been pulled on board by their arms right up the ship's side from a canoe.   The men climbed a ladder, but the women dared not do so, and had to be dragged by their arms.   When the infant of one of these women was handed up to a sailor on deck, the mother showed no interest or anxiety.   I never saw people who seemed to be so poor and so like animals. I was told that when their beasts die of disease or of old age they eat the flesh with the formula, "God cut it for us." They build and ornament with paint their beautiful wooden houses, none of which we saw. The chief of the particular tribe to whom these people belonged had died about three months ago, but his obsequies were still being celebrated. Three hundred buffaloes and three thousand pigs and many thousands of chickens had been killed to help him on his unearthly way.

We landed at Paloppo in the evening; the air was very warm and had the green smell of a hot-house.

The following day we consulted the Resident and other people about our journey as far as Leboni. They all repeated the warnings which we had already heard. In Paloppo was staying Mynheer Salm, the Comptroller of Masamba, a place forty-five miles away, and he took us in his motor to Masamba through uninteresting scenery and intense heat. Talbot arrived with high fever, which raged for three days, and we almost decided to give up the hard mountainous way which, however, offered us our best chance of getting a bos anoa, and lay amongst interesting aborigines. Another route to the north was easier, but it was well known, and was less alluring.

The Comptroller at Masamba, not being married, lived in the Rest House. He was half Javanese and half Dutch. He used to cook the evening meal, which we ate alone together, he being clothed in pyjamas. When talking he would sometimes kick off his sandals, emphasising his conversation by gesticulating with his naked feet. He never asked if Talbot was getting better. At first he was shy and defiant, but I spoke soft words to him, because I pitied him. He was lonely, for there were no Dutch people in Masamba. The servants did not keep the house clean or give him good food. His jurisdiction extended to a village beyond Leboni, but he had never been into the hills, although it was his duty to go as far as Leboni once a year. He said he would follow us if we did go by that way. He revealed to me that he did not know even the outline of the Life of Christ, in spite of having been schooled in Holland.

Masamba was an odd place. It had many white roads and was the last outpost with a road. In a rough compound used as a prison about one hundred country people were suffering punishment, because they refused to work on these roads for the compulsory forty-two days each year. Others were imprisoned because they would not grow rice, coffee and vegetables, but preferred to live on sago which grew at their doors in noble palms that needed no tending. The Netherlands' Government said : " You will have skin diseases, and be weak and lazy, if you eat only sago," and prison was the outcome of the different outlook on what is desirable.

CHAPTER XXII

CROSSING CELEBES

"Sweat and be saved."
ROOSEVELT.

ON the third day the fever left Talbot.

On the fourth day we started at six o'clock in the morning, determined to go to Leboni, thence through the jungle, and on past Toraja villages to Posso. The jungle part of our journey was in no-man's land, for it lay between the districts of two Comptrollers, one Mynheer Salm of Masamba, and the other the official at Posso. As neither Comptroller ever needed to cross the jungle, and nobody else wanted to do so, it was virgin ground. Mynheer Salm had arranged with a Chief to go with us right through past Leboni and beyond the jungle as far as the village of Manoewana, which came under the authority of the Resident at Posso. The Chief was to take three ponies, one for himself and one for each of us, the hire of which we paid. The porters whom he would engage, compulsorily if necessary, would be paid a very small stipulated sum for each mile—I think a penny a mile.

We had nineteen men with us, seven for the food and baggage, and twelve for a chair which Mynheer

Salm insisted must go with us in case Talbot, who was weak, should need it on the way. The people of Masamba are not strong and hardy, or used to carrying weights. They carried our boxes, about eighty pounds weight, slung on a great bamboo, with a man at each end. Eight men carried the chair, the other four being relays, but we used the chair hardly at all. I was carried in it for a short time, but hated the clumsy contrivance, with the sighing, sweating men. Our Tomacacque or Chief was an immense man, half Bugis and half Toraja. He spoke Malay, Bugis and the dialects of the villages we would go through, of which one, named Rantemanock, was our first stopping place.

We followed in single file a narrow green trail, the beauty of which was entrancing. We passed the graceful sago palm, and the noble wine palm, and a palm the like of which I never had seen before. Its stem was as a snake and it grew corkscrew-fashion, shotting out green at each half-circle. We saw also a fern that grew in geometrical shapes. In some places there had been landslips, but where the rocks had been hurtled down the hillsides tender ferns had risen up and healed the gashes. Here and there, in spaces amid the hills, rice had been sown. Enjoying the beauty of the vegetation, we ascended gently fifteen miles of trail to the hamlet of the Rantemanock. As we neared the village we heard the rush of a turbulent river, over which the plucky little stallions were swum, whilst we had to climb into a huge tree from which was swung a plaited bamboo bridge some eighty yards long. It

THE BRIDGE IN THE TREES.

Photographs by J. Talbot Clifton.

THE TOMACACQUE.

To face page 230.

ended in the branches of another great tree. This bridge was built by natives for natives. Each of us went alone and the bridge swayed dangerously. Our passage was made less difficult by a narrow plank laid along its length. Had either of us fallen, the basket sides of the bridge must surely have broken.

At Rantemanock was an old, old man, who did not at all know his age, nor could any other count his years. He remembered only that he had known all the inhabitants of the village, either as little children or as people younger than himself. He wished us well as we sat and ate in the stockaded village whence a new batch of men was allotted to us for the carrying of the baggage. These men of the mountains were used to weights, and each one carried forty pounds on his shoulders, with a supporting strap going round his forehead. The boxes were folded in covers of rough palm fibre. We ate and slept that night at Seba, eight miles from Rantemanock.

Seba had a running river. The Tomacacque, swathed in white draperies, lay beside it on a bed of palms that the men had cut for him. I had pitted my will against his, and fought against his unfruitful word *biasa*—" the custom." It was *biasa* that all horses should have sore backs at the end of a journey, *biasa* that their saddle cloths should be taken off as soon as ever they arrived at a halting place. I tried to teach him that this way was wrong. He had the trappings taken off his horse as soon as we reached Seba, but I would have my way about the two animals we were hiring. I loosened the saddles, took them off half an hour later, left the numnahs on even longer, and finally dried the ponies' backs with grass. Then, obstinate and contented, I rested. At the end of our journey our ponies had sound backs while his had the predestined sore back—*biasa*.

We bathed in the river and ate our evening meal. I felt a horrid fear because Talbot was tired and had a strange swelling under his tongue. I thought how awesome it would be if he fell ill. How should I get him through Celebes and how tend him ? Would the men desert us in the jungle ? Could I master the gross and ignorant Tomacacque ? The Explorer would have mocked had I told him my thoughts, for to have any doubts or fears on a journey is to him as ill-timed as to be niddering on a campaign. The road to follow and the point to gain ; these are what matter. The rest is nothing.

Thus with a day of beauty behind us, and with fear in my mind, close to the river, in the valley of the hills of Seba, we slept away the first night of our marching towards Leboni.

CHAPTER XXIII

SEBA TO LEO THROUGH MASARONG

> " Allons-nous en par la terre,
>   Sur nos deux chevaux charmants,
>   Dans l'azur, dans la mystère,
>   Dans les éblouissements ! "
>
> VICTOR HUGO.

AFTER toasting Aurora in a cup of cocoa and not other-wise breaking our fast, we rode this day some twenty-two miles past Masarong to Leo.   Masarong, yes—but why Masarong ?—for there was nothing to name save a stream and a wretched bamboo bivouac, and yet Masarong with " a name of its own and a place in the world no doubt," must have had some character, otherwise I should not have disliked it as I did.   We waited there for our carriers, who came long after we were rested.   'Bros had delayed them by sleeping during the march.   He was a feeble traveller, and later on he became a bye-word for sleep.   We never stopped anywhere without his sleeping immediately, regardless of the duty he had to perform.   Camp beds might wait to be put up, food might wait to be cooked, but 'Bros must sleep.   Later on in our journey he used to sleep whilst walking, and thus often hurt his feet against twigs or on stones.

By the stream near the bridge we ate bacon, and we

were glad when the carriers chose to continue the march as far as Leo, 4,500 feet up in the hills, rather than spend the night at Masarong. The trail grew narrower after we left Masarong and it circled above steep precipices that lay sheer down one side of it. No rice fields were now to be seen, but only immense trees and palms; a few flowers gladdened us. Great precipices gaped below. The jungle in these highlands was unchanging. The last two miles of climbing were too steep to ride. Again we arrived before the carriers; the evening fell, and the rain. When the men arrived, I washed their feet and legs with balm, as all of them had cuts and bruises. This help gave them great joy; they were too child-like to do anything for themselves. Then we supped. We lent the Tomacacque one of our leather pig-skin coats, and we lay in the frail bamboo shelter shivering under a few coverings, whilst the mists and the breezes and the rain came through the bamboo hut. The gallant carriers huddled round a fire in the open below us, every man naked save for odd pieces of stuff. So passed the frigid night on the heights of Leo.

CHAPTER XXIV

LEO TO DOLOLO THROUGH LEBONI

"Poverty is not the result of capitalism, but the original condition of man."

H. Cox.

At half-past six next morning we set out on eighteen miles of jungle that lay before us.

We saw grey mists, flowers pale through lack of sun, and trees rotted with damp and darkness, the great turbid darkness of a too dense jungle. The horrid cold of sunless heights smote us. Dying trees were shrouded in grey mosses, and the brooding silence was broken only by the heavy flap of the hornbill's wings. The woods that grew up around the Sleeping Beauty—La Belle au Bois Dormant—must have been like this.

We let the coolies get in front of us, but, alas, kept coming up to them, and every time 'Bros was asleep.

Man's misery seemed here to equal the dreariness of the rotting trees, for the only signs of his passing were strange traps. "What are they for?" I asked the Tomacacque. "To catch rats, which the people eat," he said.

Two hours after the sun had shown us the midday

we came out from the jungle into a plain with long, warm, waving grass amongst which grew orchids, the terrestrial purple anceps. Low hills lay about us, and we rode down and down into a valley, then suddenly we entered a palisaded village. This was Leboni. A large house on mighty wooden pillars, the people's House of Talk, was in the centre of the village, and now from the lesser houses many women came out to welcome us. I am not sure if I was the first white woman they had seen. I think that a Dutch woman had been in Leboni before me. Upon their heads the women wore bands of reed painted and silvered over, and bodices of red, white and blue. Trailing skirts, made from the bark of trees woven into a fabric that looked like coarse brown calico, were gathered into bustles behind them. The women seemed strangely early-Victorian with their straightened hair, formal and old-fashioned, like prim housekeepers, and this in spite of their faces being painted in black with stars and crosses and squares. Their men had almost nothing on but a loincloth or small white shorts, with an amusing little sporran made from sapi-utan skins. They looked especially naked beside the much-dressed tall and dignified women.

The women crowded round my pony to shake hands. Two or three of them would put up their cold, limp hands into one of mine.

We then rode on to an empty house kept for the Comptroller, though he had never been here. The coolies had arrived an hour before us, but 'Bros had prepared nothing; this was enraging.

MEN OF LEBONI.

WOMEN OF LEBONI.

To face page 236.

After settling him down to cook, I attended to the men's feet, then, just as I was going to bathe in the river, the Comptroller arrived. We had done the fifty-four miles' journey in three days, eighteen miles each day, and found that enough of walking and riding, though not too much. We could ride only at walking pace, for the horses are very small, we very big, and the path narrow and often steep. But Mynheer Salm had done twenty-seven miles a day, and the whole journey in two days. One pony he had exhausted utterly, and had shot it on the road. His carriers, who arrived hours later, were worn out. He bathed, but found the water too cold and did not brave it again during the next three days we spent together. There were no basins in these Rest Houses, so that the river was the only means of cleanliness.

We all dined on fried chicken and rice, whilst the people of the village danced slowly before us, giving us baskets of rice and of eggs. The Comptroller interviewed some of the people, speaking to them through the Tomacacque. He was clothed in pyjamas, and when he wanted to attract the Tomacacque's attention, he kicked that Chief's black leg softly with his naked foot. When his carriers came he threw into the dust before them the wages they had so hardly earned.

At seven o'clock we all went to our camp beds.

The next day we spent in Leboni. Sloping hills frame it, but these are clothed with grasses instead of with trees, though in the villages are palms and bamboos. A man from the Minahassa was living near the village experimenting in coffee-growing on behalf of the government, and he, in time, would teach the people the uses of various plants and crops new to them.

The women of Leboni put on their ceremonial dresses that we might photograph them. They wore fine woven stuffs patterned like Russian cloths, with capes of beads fringed with metal. The men came with jackets and drawers which the man of the Minahassa had brought to them. We had to send them back to their houses till they consented to appear with flowing loin cloths, and spears and helmets, and stand before us in warrior pomp as their fathers would have stood against us.

I woke thinking : " To-day we go from Leboni to Dololo with the Tomacacque and the Comptroller, and we have only eight miles to travel." In front of us went the Explorer with his rifle, and a party of men of Leboni with dogs and spears, to hunt the elusive sapi-utan. Painfully in the plain they hunted, amid the long, impeding grasses, where here and there grew flowering trees like elm trees. Talbot saw a speeding form and took a snapshot at it, with his ·240 Holland rifle. He feared that he had not mortally wounded it. Now the men and dogs outdistanced him, the men calling out : " You have hit the beast ; we will pursue it through the long grasses."

When we reached Dololo together, the people of the village again gave us presents of welcome, and we gave them beads and silver paper. I cooked dried

THE MEN THAT, WITH TALBOT, HUNTED THE BOS-ANOA.

Photographs by J. Talbot Clifton.

THE BULLS OF BALI.

To face page 238.

beans and rice for the next day's journey, and laid the supper table with a fair cloth of banana leaves. We supped splendidly off wild teal that had been brought in. Rice fields encircled us. A noble looking headman of North American Indian type watched over the ponies, whilst I again observed how different the type of the primitive aristocrat is from the type of the primitive lesser man. I could promise to mark out the chieftain by his face and carriage in any of the villages of the islands through which we journeyed.

At sunset the hunting party came in with the fine bos anoa that had been shot by Talbot. This had been found by the dogs some little way further in the bush. The party had delayed its return, hoping to kill a second beast. By the light of the lamp, we looked at the rare creature, the first of this species, as far as we know, that had ever been shot by an Englishman. For years scientists were doubtful whether to call it an antelope, buffalo, or ox, but have decided now that whilst there are ox-like antelopes, such as the gnu and eland, so in the sapi-utan is a buffalo which is akin to the antelope. For a buffalo, it is small, the smallest indeed of the wild oxen. It is delicately made, its skin of a fine texture; its horns a foot long, straight and smooth, ringed at the base and lying backwards. We knew it to be full of courage, inspiring fear alike in Netherlander and Celeban. We knew that it had but seldom survived captivity, a creature the very name of which is almost unknown. Talbot now oversaw the skinning of the head, which skin was afterwards scraped to free it from fat and flesh. It was well salted, and now became my charge. I had to safeguard it from ants and accidents till we should reach the seaport of Posso. Talbot's main object in visiting the Island of Celebes was accomplished.

CHAPTER XXV

FROM DOLOLO TO MANOEWANA

> "They are *our* history, master, they are *our* old
> times. Though they be bad they are *our* times,
> master, and now they go. I am sad, master, when
> the old Gods go."
>
> LORD DUNSANY.

AT Dololo we bade the Comptroller adieu, as his jurisdiction ended here. Now the Tomacacque, with some
men from Dololo, was to take us on to the village of
Manoewana. He had never been through the jungle
that divides the villages and the two jurisdictions. The
men of Dololo knew a way they said, but we must send
the ponies back as the crossing would be too hard for
them, and they would be useless. Talbot opposed
this, and said that the ponies must come in case either
of us got fever, and so after much discussion it was
decided that they should accompany us at our own
risk.

A thrill of awe went through me as we left Dololo
for the jungle. The Tomacacque was visibly ill at
ease, not trusting the men, and not knowing anything
of the way. The men said : "We know the jungle
but little, for in Dololo is our heart's desire." From
early morning we walked till three o'clock in the afternoon, stopping twice only for a short rest. The jungle

was Gehenna, our journey uphill for some nineteen miles through a tangled blur of green, with no spaces at all. Sometimes we had to crawl sixty to seventy feet along the trunk of a fallen tree, the men being forced to cut a passage round it for the ponies to pass. These plucky animals crossed ravines and climbed like cats up steep places. All the time they were led by men who had never handled a horse before. We were not able to ride them at all.

At two o'clock the leader from Dololo stopped on a flat grassy space that, amid the encircling jungle, lay open to the rain that fell in torrents.

" Here we will spend the night," he said.

We got out our camp chairs, put up a large Chinese paper umbrella, recovered our breath, and rested our cramped and stiff limbs.

Then, " No," said Talbot, " we will go on."

We went on for an hour down into the jungle, and we came on the ruin of a native shelter near the water.

" We will stop here," Talbot said.

Gaily, after their great labour, the men now went into the thicket and cut branches of palms, wherewith they quickly built two houses. Into one we moved our beds, and the men took the second one, whilst the Tomacacque chose the old ruined hut, full of wild bees. Talbot took photographs and I bathed the men's legs, which were covered with leeches and blood. The sun came out, and we dried our clothes in its glory, and fried some sapi-utan that tasted like tough beef. The sun set, the cold night entered the jungle. Then we slept profoundly.

"THEY BUILT HOUSES OF PALM-BRANCHES."

Photographs by J. Talbot Clifton.

ONE OF OUR PONIES.

To face page 242.

Next day was Friday. We prepared to leave our beautiful hut that I loved. Talbot grumbled a little because of the uphill posture of his bed, caused by its being on a slope. I found dressing difficult, as the men kept coming in for their packs. To wash was impossible. As a description of the day's travel I shall copy what Talbot wrote to a friend :

" This day's march was a repetition of the former, excepting that the climbing was more precipitous and the track more indistinguishable than the day before. This day my guide had to help me up many horrible ascents. Towards the afternoon we saw glimpses of cultivated land, and thus we emerged from the darkest and most inaccessible heart of Celebes to a native village, from whence there is a well-engineered path one hundred and twenty miles to the sea."

When we came forth from the jungle we had to push our way through long grasses, and through bracken that grew up to our eyes. Terrestrial orchids bloomed before us, the Spathoglottis plicata, a purple anceps. Save for just the last mile we could not ride at all. Although that day we had only travelled ten miles we were tired when we reached Manoewana, and glad to go to the Rest House, there to find a man from Posso who spoke Malay. He was here called a " Mandri," whom the Comptroller of Posso had sent to interpret for us. The Tomacacque was to return home with his ponies, and we were to hire other carriers. Our house was of palm, it stood above the pretty village with its many palms. The children sang and danced in the street, and women moved about, but they lacked the grandeur of the matrons of Leboni, and looked like cinderellas with their bunched-up skirts of wood bark.

I changed my clothes and we supped. Before the day's end the Chief of the village, who was a Christian, called upon us. Half the villagers were heathen and the other half were Christian; the Chief's brother was not baptised. The Chief had a fine face, resembling that of a Red Indian, though the other people were of almost negroid type. This headman's face showed expression and his eyes shone with enquiry, the rarest of emotions for an Easterner. He had with him his daughter Lolé, who was about thirteen years of age. She was pretty, the first lovely face I had seen in all Celebes. It lit with pleasure when I gave her some beads. Her sister's face was ugly with black squares and crosses. Then I had a vision of Lolé's future. She will be sold to a husband for many buffaloes. She will make her clothes from the bark of trees and take a month to weave an ugly garment. She will work hard in the fields with her husband, but she will not work harder than he. She will never leave her children, and even when they are big they will never leave her. Often she will sing all the night through, and dance, moving in strange figures and slow cadences. She will not be troubled about money, or about her soul, or about anything at all, for even if sickness comes she will accept it without trying to fight it, as we accept bad weather, a matter beyond control.

I was the first white woman here, but, alas, I inspired

horror. The Chief, I could see, thought me monstrous, not physically perhaps, but morally, because I had left my children, my pretty babes, whose photographs I showed him. I showed him one of Lytham Hall also. He could not understand why a house should be so large, nor how it could be built of hard brick squares instead of bamboo. But he understood less the hard block that my heart must be if I could leave my children. I told him that we left England because Talbot was ill, and I felt I must go with him, but that I missed my five beloveds very much. Two or three times he said : " You should have brought them." I blushed under the scorn of his eyes. Then they went away, he and pretty Lolé, out of my life for ever, but not out of my memory.

The moon shone, the stars came out, the night was full of sound until the dawn of day. " Elloi, Elloi, Elloi " a man chanted, or words that sounded like that, and this for half an hour or more, then the words changed and other voices sang, or intoned on two notes, C and D, I thought they were. Now and again, alone in the woods, I can repeat these queer notes, and then as suddenly I lose them. The women sang with voices like boys, whilst the men beat on drums and blew on pipes. They all marched and danced in coiling figures like the letter S. I lay on my camp bed and listened spellbound, for repetition has a curious effect, hypnotic or psychic I know not, but I know that a kind of exaltation is its product. I knew afterwards that the concourse sang of the price of women, the great buffaloes that are counted out as her price, of the coming of the white man, of the dreary infliction of road-making, of the protection given by the new law to wicked witches who may no longer be killed, and of how the white man can out-bid the dark man for the village maidens.   At last I slept. . . .

"TERRESTRIAL ORCHIDS BLOOMED" SPATHOGLOTTIS PLICATA.

To face page 246.

CHAPTER XXVI

MANOEWANA TO BESOA THROUGH GINTO AND LELIO

"O memory, take and keep all that my eyes, your servants, bring you home."

EDWARD SHANKS.

THE next day, the 12th August, we rode twelve miles on the Tomacacque's ponies, for he was to leave us at Ginto, from whence he had heard of a way across the jungle back to his home, a way far easier than the track which the men of Dololo had cut for us. The existence of the road that the Tomacacque now took had been unknown to us, although a Missionary had used it. No man had ever travelled the way we came. We rode along a good grassy path through rich tableland country. We passed a deserted village left empty, as no rice could be grown there, but the other villages were as pretty as gardens, and each had a school and a Malay-speaking teacher from the Minahassa. A Lutheran form of Christianity is gradually taking root here. We passed over another great swinging bridge, far longer and more primitive than the first, for it was one hundred and fifty yards long. It sagged in the middle, and the foothold was only four bamboos tied together, about as broad as four fingers. We had

247

again to climb up into a tree, and into this basket bridge, under which a torrential river ran. The ponies went lower down the river and swam over. Thus, adventurously, we reached the valley of Ginto—the loveliest place on the long journey across Celebes.

Here was a river and hills. Jolly children played to us on flutes. Talbot shot teal, which 'Bros and I, like dogs, retrieved by plunging into the river. That night we cooked and ate our spoil.

Next day we said farewell to the good black Tomacacque ; jocund was he and pleasant. As he looked at the plump and cheerful stallions that we now returned to him, then at the sore and sorry beast that he had ridden, he owned that I had been wise in my care of our animals. Whether he afterwards imitated my cunning I cannot tell.

When we travelled on towards Leone we had new ponies, and rode uphill until we reached a plateau. In a letter Talbot describes our journey thus : " Whilst travelling through the heart of Celebes I observed a most interesting feature, namely, three plains each with rich soil, each inhabited, and each encircled by mountains, and each plain about 2000 feet above sea level."

Our Mandri told me of the Orang Alfuros, to which belong those of the Lorée tribe with the Lorée language, the men of Bada, Bomba, Besoa, and Napoe. Further North came the Orang Barée, who are of another tribe and language, and to this tribe belong the people of Posso and neighbouring places. The further name of Toraja I understood applied to them all.

We passed a Mission House at Bomba and reached Lelio, where we tarried overnight. Before resting, Talbot sought teal along the river bank, bordered by rice fields, whilst I baked bread and washed clothes.

Next day we covered thirty kilometres between Lelio and Besoa. We arrived at Besoa at half-past one. I suffered because my pony had a sore mouth. The bits given us at Lelio were barbarous, all jagged and spiked. We had no saddles, but Talbot had stirrups of cord arranged over a sack. Through miles of jungle we rode, then passed a plateau where was no village. We lunched near a bridge roofed with bamboos, a shelter for wayfarers. We had expected to use such shelter at night, but we never did so.

On that day Talbot's Guardian Angel again proved his power—how often has he warded death away from one who never shuns danger ! We were riding along a rugged little path overhanging a sheer precipice of about one thousand feet, at the bottom of which a torrential river ran. Talbot was immediately in front of me. I had just been thinking, " If one of these horses shied and missed its footing, we should change our world," when suddenly Talbot's stallion stiffened. It stood stark and trembling. We saw the tail of a snake slithering down into some bushes below. Fortunately, the horse did not swerve. Strange that later on, another snake passed in almost exactly the same manner in front of Talbot, who always led us. This time the stallion took no notice of the reptile. Our Mandri told us that the second snake was not poisonous ; the horse must therefore have known which was venomous and which was harmless.

When we arrived at Besoa the Mandri told us that we had passed some ancient ruins, though he could not tell us much about them. I was troubled at having gone past something strange and ancient without having seen it. Then he somewhat solaced me by saying that there were also old curious remains near Besoa. " Are they there by God's will or by man's ? " I asked, meaning, " Are they of Nature or are they man-made ? " " Neither the one nor the other," he answered seriously. " Iblis is said to have made them." By which he meant the Devil. I told him I would visit them on the morrow.

The path we had followed was well planned, it had been made by order of the Netherlands' Government, but the natives themselves had engineered it. This surprised Talbot, who had thought it was of European construction, as it showed real scientific design and execution.

Tired with our journey we put up our camp beds and slept—'Bros as usual feigning, or suffering, illness.

So stiff and sore was I after many days of marching, that it needed will power on the next day to go off the necessary way to seek what, from the Mandri's description, I was beginning to think must be tombs. We started away in the morning, making for the place where the monuments were said to be. For seven miles we thrust our way through long spear grasses, whilst the sun tormented us. Suddenly came

THE WELLS OF BESOA

To face page 250.

the crown of endeavour. With quickened breath, I beheld the great monuments. Had they been wells ? They were not deep enough to have held much water. Had they been treasuries for wealth, or tombs of the mighty ?

There were ten of them, made of grey stone, though there was no trace of rocks for miles and miles. The biggest was six feet high, and four feet deep ; some were only one foot deep. They had great covers of stone measuring five yards round, but some of the covers had been taken away, and trees were springing up out of the stone. Upon two of these covers apes were carved in bold relief, and on another was the figure of a recumbent woman.

No one knows their history ; no European had ever, I think, visited them. I tried to imagine a race of perished people who had perhaps used these mighty receptacles for storing treasure. So strange and foreign were the ruins that only Iblis could have formed them ; that was what the Mandri thought. It did not seem foolish to me as I scanned them there in the hot plain amid the cutting grasses.

We returned slowly. The romance of the mysterious wells of Besoa glowed within me.

CHAPTER XXVII

FROM BESOA THROUGH WATOETOE, SIDOEPA, NANGEA AND PINIIDAPA TO POSSO

" It's a long way to go."

FROM Besoa to Watoetoe, a distance of thirty-three kilometres, our carriers went very slowly and arrived hours after we did. At Besoa I first noticed a coolie with skin roughened like the scales of a fish. This is the sign of a skin disease called tinea circinata. I did not at the time recognise it as being ringworm. The treatment which would cure the sufferers is a slow one, and they seldom submit to it, nor did they regard the malady in their friends other than as amusing. They laughed a great deal when I allocated the carrying of our bath to the diseased man, because I thought this article was the most easily cleansed of infection. Dr. Van der Veer told me that he avoided as much as possible touching people so afflicted. In hospital, this caution on his part was the cause of merriment.

I reckoned that one out of every twelve of our escort had the disease. The inhabitants of this part of Celebes seemed to me, after the massive and virile Bugis, to be both listless and ill. We saw many of them with framboesia or yaws, and were told that

ninety per cent. of the villagers suffer from this dis-
temper. The injection called 606 [1] because Dr.
Ehrlich tried six hundred and six times before he
perfected it, is a cure for this tedious illness and the
Celebans travel many days to receive the painful treatment. " Mynworm " or ankylostom duodenalis is
another very common form of suffering. This worm,
about half an inch long, can penetrate the human body
in a variety of ways, but is supposed by doctors here to
enter mainly by the bare feet of the natives and then to
lay its eggs. The disease causes anæmia, dropsy, and
every form of indigestion, including dirt-eating. All
soldiers are attended for this, and once the worm is
removed the soldiers become so strong and well that it
costs twice as much to feed them ! We saw some eye
illness too, but not so much as in some other parts of
the East.

This day we again rode through the jungle, and
finally we emerged into a rich valley, with people
working in the ripe corn, the women crowned with
bands of palm wood oddly painted. At a distance
they looked charming.

While I rode I was amused by a native assistant, a
man of Menado, who came to meet us. He was
delighted by our pig-skin coats, which caused astonishment in various parts of Celebes. He asked me a lot
about Europe. Usually the folk of Celebes showed no
interest at all in hearing about that continent, but he
asked me many questions. At last he remarked :

[1] Later modified but doubtfully improved, although more fool-
proof to 914.

" People here eat and sleep and are happy as long as their bowels work, but Europeans think."

" What enormous beehives ! " I cried suddenly, gazing in astonishment at structures of bamboo set on piles. Then I saw that they were the dwellings of the people.

In a letter to my children I thus described Watoetoe : " Children, if you lived in Watoetoe, you would have for a home a kind of beehive, a hut on wooden legs, with all four sides of the roof right down to the floor ; just a square for the window, just a square for the door, and a pole with notches for a staircase, and dead darkness inside. Your mother would cook rice amidst lots of smoke, and your father would have long hair tied up in a handkerchief. There would be insects in everyone's head. Your mother would wear a short skirt of bark, and a kind of jumper of painted woven bark ; the jumper and the skirt would have a gap and show her tummy in between. Your father would wear a few, very dirty clothes. More than likely, some of you would have skin disease. Your father and mother would neither read nor write, but you would go to school and learn Malay, for without that language no one outside your own village would understand you. You would probably go to the Lutheran service on Sunday and your parents would gradually become Christian, to please the kind missionary. Secretly, you would think a lot about the devil, and when you ate food, you would throw aside the first mouthful for him. Your father, on being told by the missionary about God, would beg : ' But please tell me about the devil.' "

My memories of the village of Watoetoe are un-pleasing. The Rajah and his wife were not helpful, though picturesque enough with red scarves and sashes. We could not procure chickens to eat or ponies to ride, and the village seemed, like Rurukan, "impertinent." The Rest House was full of un-necessary mosquitoes, insects from which the country is very free, and which would not have been there had the house been cleaned. When I reproved the "tuan," or headman, he merely said : " They are God's own creatures," and left it at that. The villagers were suffering from unstable minds, tossed between Christi-anity misunderstood and a remnant of heathen lore. The people respected neither us nor themselves.

We lived two days at Watoetoe, detained by rain and the difficulty of getting ponies and saddles ; then we left on foot, which was a relief to me as I hate riding sore backed animals. We walked twenty-eight kilo-metres to Sidoepa, through country not unlike English downs. After reaching the summit of the hills we descended into the jungle. The palm hut where we spent the night was pleasant enough ; a pool in the river, full of mint and thyme, was delicious ; but I was hungry, and in my diary noted that alas! these delights made me think only of roast lamb. 'Bros was nearly always ill with fever, which meant that I must cook our supper after the long day's march.

Next day we went from Sidoepa to Nangea, covering sixteen kilometres of great beauty. Our way lay down-hill, yet the march seemed long. Our night's shelter was dirty, and the men's hut, which was opposite to ours, was all open to the cold night and the mists.   We had walked all day on the trail that the souls follow on their way to the hills of Nappo.   The souls of the dead, both good and evil, are all equal when the body is shed, and they travel along to Nappo—as we did.   When they arrive amid the hills of Nappo, they eat and drink and laugh for ever.   If any man gets lost in the jungle, his friends think that the devil has misled him, and no one tries to find him ;   yet in this trackless maze of green what more easy than to get lost ?

Nangea was beautiful and mysterious ;   there were no birds, butterflies, animals or flowers ;   just the jungle and the great solitary trees.

I mused on Emerson's saying :   " As a plant upon the earth, so a man rests upon the bosom of God ;   he is fed by innumerable fountains, and draws at his need inexhaustible power." [1]   I had tried hard to attain power, and had attained it, but I was immensely tired. A sort of exaltation had carried me on.   The excitement of a new life had buoyed me up.   It was an adventure to test my endurance in the hills and through the densities, in the great heat of the plains, and the chill of the heights.   The Explorer had started forth feverish and weak, but gradually was growing strong ; I was coming to the end of my possibilities.   I think it is so with men and women ;   men increase in strength, whilst women put their all into one effort, then become exhausted and fail.   Anyway my shoes were wearing out and were tied to my feet with pieces of rattan.

[1] I quote from memory.

The night closed over Nangea and we slept.

'Bros told us that he was as ill as on the day before. We started from Nangea toward Piniidapa, without taking his temperature. I was troubled exceedingly, for I thought he might die, but Talbot said he was not " leading a nursery party," that I was foolish to be so concerned and to take pains over the weights each man carried; the men were able to look after themselves. He was right, for when we had been in Piniidapa for an hour, and I had lighted the fire and cooked some bacon, 'Bros came in half asleep with no temperature at all.

The village people looked at us with inflamed and running eyes, which the Mandri told us would get worse at the season of husking the rice and corn. The boys played with a big fruit stone, at which they threw other stones by means of a string, the game being to touch with their small missiles this centre stone whilst it was still spinning.

The leeches had been legion for nearly all the twenty kilos, so that the men needed much tending. Talbot and I did not much mind the bite of leeches.

Towards the end of the journey the path was carpeted with delicate, sensitive plants, the verdure of which entirely blotted out the trail. As our feet bruised them the plants folded up, revealing the pathway.

We had one pony which we rode in turns during the last twenty kilos of our journey. Our way lay at first through long grass, and some difficult little plank bridges had to be crossed. The leeches were again " very plenty," as say the people of Connemara.

The heat on nearing Posso was excessive, and we looked utterly disreputable as we entered the town. Our shoes were torn, our khaki worn and crumpled, our carriers and ourselves bleeding with leech bites. The Arab merchants gathered at their shop-doors scanned us with evident scorn, but the Chinese merchant veiled his contempt.

I looked forward to seeing Mrs. Van der Veer and the doctor. The thought of the comfort of their home solaced my fatigue, for they had said we were to go to them on our return to Posso. Alas ! we were met by a bearer of bad news, who said that an epidemic had broken out somewhere near ; the doctor had had to go to the afflicted village, and therefore Mrs. Van der Veer could not receive us. So would we use the Mission House ?

If cleanliness is next to godliness then, as Talbot remarked, these worthy missionaries had not much hope of salvation, for the house was dirtier than any of the shelters we had used for our crossing. Ants covered everything. Instead of the rude simplicity of a bamboo hut, we found a European house with dirty fittings and soiled curtains, and a pile of plates for us to wash before we could even have a meal.

'Bros was ill, and I cried when I saw the horrid house, and knew we must abide there for several days before the steamer came.

From Masamba, our last Europeanized post, we had come 220 miles on foot and on pony, travelling through the jungle along a track never before used by Europeans.

WE TWO AND OUR MEN AT THE END OF THE CROSSING OF CELEBES.

A HOUSE IN WATOETOE.

To face page 258.

From the coast of Masamba we had travelled forty-five miles by motor, so that the total journey from South to North Celebes was 265 miles. We left Masamba on August 6, and arrived at Posso on August 23. We had seen vast table-lands and plentiful harvesting; jungles and primitive peoples, and had secured a sapi-utan. Because Talbot and I had spent ourselves getting that strange little trophy, the sapi-utan's head, it was one of the few things that I took with me when, later, rebels forced me within some numbered hours to leave Connemara.

CHAPTER XXVIII

THE EAST COAST

"Happy too is he who knows the woodland gods, Pan
and old Silvanus and the sister nymphs."
Georgics.—Virgil.

We were now to return to Macassar round by the east
coast of Celebes ; indeed all our days had been arranged
to fit in with this plan. There was no time-table
connection, but the K.P.M. Company had magnani-
mously promised that the s.s. *St. Jacob* should await
us at Gorontalo, whither the s.s. *Linschoten* would
take us from Posso. The *Linschoten* came to Posso
three days late, so we had no hope of finding the *St.
Jacob* ; but, in a hurricane of rain, we did with surprise
see her gladdening form, and joyously boarded her,
and were greeted by Captain Roelleveld. To open our
eyes in the mornings on days that did not each demand
a fifteen mile march, and to know we would have
bread and fresh food, that was very good.

We steamed away past the bold headlands that
guard the Gorontalo River, going south in a blur of
rain that did not cease till we dropped anchor that
evening. We waited till the morning following to
enter the port of Bangaya, for in these inadequately
charted seas great care, as well as many risks, must be

THE ALBINO.

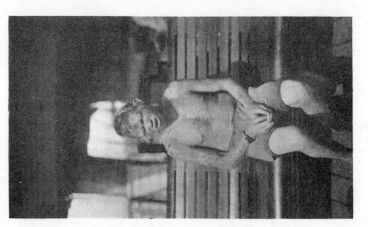

Photographs by J. Talbot Clifton.

EAST COAST CELEBANS.

To face page 260.

taken by the captains. Bangaya is the port for the Peling group of isles which are opposite the Sula Isles. Our morning there is burnt into my brain.

Upon landing we went up to the small barracks, for this part of Eastern Celebes has not yet reached the era of Comptrollers and Residents, but is still perforce under military management. In the barracks I saw a thing revolting, the unclothed albino child of a dark-skinned race. His skin looked like the skin of a dying dog-fish. It was greenish grey and spotted. He was monstrous, unnatural; probably he suffered. With his unpigmented, unresisting skin, he must have been martyred by the scorching sun; he seemed to be half imbecile.

Then I saw four captives. The first of them was lovely beyond praise, a golden pigeon in a cage. We were told that its kind lives only in Bangaya. It shimmered like copper. I understood in a gasp how Greek gods delighted in assuming animal forms; this glorious body might worthily have clothed any celestial being. The other three prisoners were loathsome. They were men. They came from Sula. They had horrible eyes; they looked both cowardly and cruel. They had committed many murders, one man having four deaths upon his hands, all murders of a degrading nature, and for a paltry gain. They had carried out their deeds with forethought and dexterity. Captain Roelleveld of the *St. Jacob* did not like taking them on board to convey them to the jail in Macassar, because he said they would be likely to let themselves die of hunger rather than arrive there as prisoners. The island, he told us, was full of drunkards and murderers. We took on no cargo. These depraved human beings were the only exports from Peling.

The Dutch officer in charge of the garrison was a blue-eyed boy physically typical of his race. He lived in this gruesome island, married to a Javanese wife. His four Eurasian children played on the verandah, and his sole link with Europe, with mails, with ice, with bread and beer, was the brief visit of the *St. Jacob* once a month.

The gentle south-west monsoon companioned us along this wondrous coast, in parts reminding us of the Scottish Highlands, and in parts of Norway. In other places the scenery was purely tropic, with forests of noble teak trees. Their branches were weighted with great flowering trusses, with mighty seed pods and noble leaves. Teak to the planter yields a delayed and tardy harvest, for it gives no return of wealth for a hundred years.

That day we saw wild pig, and monkeys which hurled cries at us. Paroquets flew by. When night fell flares were lit, and by these our ship was guided to safe anchorage opposite the village of Kolonedale in the Bay of Tomori. In the light of the infant moon our anchor was dropped. This was the vigil to one of the most beneficent days I have lived. The day dawned in fullest beauty. With great skill our ship was navigated out of the sea lake. We were banked in by mountains five or six thousand feet high. It often seemed as though our course was blocked by a rocky island rising out of the sea ; then the azure way would again thread out before us. Some of the islets grew like mushrooms with slim stalks of rock in the sea. Poor Echo of the Legend had made her home in this bay; at noon she four times repeated one call of the ship's siren.

After a day of beatitude, of sunrise and still seas, of mountains and rocks, of grace and of immensity, we anchored near Sakita, a place of tragic memory. Fourteen years before a Dutch officer and fourteen soldiers had been killed treacherously and cut into fragments by the people. Here we found a Dutch girl, delicious as a hyacinth, married to the dark Eurasian military officer. I bethought me of the pleasant boy from Holland with the Javanese wife, who lived just north of her, and I longed to remarry them. East to East and West to West. This Desdemona saddened me.

The last four days of our cruise have left in my mind only a series of outlines. There was Kendari, on the mainland, with a row of houses built on stakes, over the sea, whilst in the main street deer that the Chinese merchants had tamed ran eagerly up and down, perhaps inspiring with their grace an added lightness of touch to the Chinese workmen who here produced fine filigree work in gold.

There was a fountain, that surprised me, as I had not seen one in Celebes, and above it was a gigantic cactus, the flowering spike of which bowed over in a sweep of eighteen feet or more.

At the next port, we did not land, but took on a cargo of stag's antlers for industry to turn into buttons. Also we took on rattan of the finer kind, to be converted into furniture, whilst the coarser kind, for which Germany had formerly been the best customer, would be used in the manufacture of explosives.

After this, we anchored off the island of Boeton or " Baoebaoe "—" bad smells." The people walked about the little town with smallpox visibly destroying them. We were joined by an Australian, Mr. H., who had dressed his servant, a man of the island, in a European knickerbocker suit, and had taught him the English language, which surprising combination of achievements greatly impressed the captain and officers of the ship. This Mr. H. was, moreover, interesting, for many years ago he had landed from a Chinese sailing ship on the island of Moena, which lies a few knots from Boeton. On that day years ago, he had wished but to tarry for an hour or so on the island of Moena. He rested and ate, then, looking up, he saw wild pig, deer, monkeys and parrots, and he thought : " This is where I shall live ; the deer and the monkeys invite me—I have found my home." There was no port, no house, just predestination. He put all his money into Moena, yoked great buffaloes with chains to jungle trees that he had hewn, and with this herculean plough the spear grass was broken down so that it withered. Then he planted a creeper to run over where the five-foot grass had been, and afterwards he planted coconuts on these flats.

The spear grass of Moena is so dense that nature has had to make a distinct invention because of it. On this

HERCULEAN PLOUGH AND SPEAR GRASS.

To face page 264.

island a curious wild pig has developed bristles under its eyes as a protection against the sword-like blades of grass.

Pulo Gala Island was our last port of call—a very small busy island, whence coconuts and rattan were shipped. The Bugis population makes sails of palm. Here I met a dark-skinned man with blue eyes, and was told that he had come from an island north of Timor, where 300 years ago was a Dutch garrison. Through many generations the blue eyes of the Netherland race had gone down looking out on the tropic world, persisting when all other physical traits, and perhaps all mental ones, had been swamped by the Malay blood.

So ended our odyssey of Celebes, on which island be peace and plenty for ever !

CHAPTER XXIX

THE ISLAND OF SUMBAWA

"Black lacqueys at the wide-flung door
    Stand mute as men of wood.
    Gleams like a pool the ball-room floor—
A burnished solitude."

WALTER DE LA MARE.

TEN days we passed in the island of Sumbawa.
Many people had said to us : " Do not go there ; it is
of no interest ; it is very hot, you will have no comfort.
There is no good road through it," but Talbot, it
seemed, had a call to Sumbawa, and though resolution
opposed by so many warnings might have faltered in
others, in him it did not. We went there.

We sailed for Bima, a port at the eastern point of
the island, spending a few days on the waters. We
had only the outline of a plan in our minds, merely
indeed the determination to cover the 145 miles from
Bima on the south-east to Port Sumbawa on the
north-east in the ten days which we had in hand
before the steamer would leave Sumbawa. We were
told that over the first forty-five miles we should be
able to travel in a motor.

We reached the Rest House and the Resident,
Mynheer ——, called on us, and was most helpful and

pleasant, saying that whatsoever we wished, that would be granted to us.

We asked if it would be possible to hunt. The next day we went off in a motor car with the Sultan of Bima —like his subjects a Bugis by race—and with the Rajah, who was the Sultan's Prime Minister. The Resident also came.

The people are Mahommedan, and together with their princely rulers, are not in a state of feeble imitation and unbeautiful transition like the people of Central Celebes, but established in their own ways, and endowed with vigorous bodies and a wealth-giving island.

The land was now all dry and baked with the sun. No rain had fallen ; even the trees were bare. After the dark density of the jungle in Celebes, it was delightful to look freely along the woodlands, and strange to see that the scorching heat had bared the bushes, as in Europe winter winds rob them of their leaves.

In a junglewood behind the hills some 2,000 men waited with spears and dogs. They had gone forth at dawn, and had driven the pigs and deer up towards the place where we were now put to wait.

For long we waited in this valley. Coconuts, bananas and oranges were laid beside the Explorer's rifle. I found pastime in watching two flowering bushes, each the counterpart of the other. On one of these lived red ants, and on the other black ants. The insects never intermixed.

Talbot wrote home about these hours of waiting :

" It interested me to note the country; there were high hills with every variety of tree and bush that carries thorns, but of undergrowth there was none, unless you include the cactus; all was dry, arid and dusty, the ground hard as iron under our feet; for this island seems to be between the great western monsoon and the gentle S.E. monsoon, the latter never touching it with its beneficent rains, the former visiting it for two months only, and that between November and January; yet Nature seemed bright and joyous and sparkling in this parched-up land, so different from the many sad and gloomy portions of Celebes." Sumbawa gave me a feeling of health and wholesomeness.

So we waited, but nothing went past us. At one o'clock we were told that the hunt was over so we rejoined the others. Fourteen deer were brought in, some speared by the huntsmen and some shot by the Sultan and the Rajah. None of them had more than six points to their antlers. The deer were carried towards us by tall men with splendid loin cloths of their wives' weaving, and with head coverings of silk run through with metal threads. Silver sheaths protected their hunting knives. Round about us stood the 2,000 beaters. Some pig had also been speared, but they were not counted or brought before us by these staunch Mahommedans.

On returning to Bima, Talbot planned our journey, the first part of which we covered next day by motor.

To help us in the villages where diverse languages are spoken, a Government clerk, a big, dark, fat man, a real Dutch-Indian Falstaff, was sent with us. " Of what country is he a native," I innocently asked the Resident. " He is a Dutchman born in the Indies," was the embarrassing reply.

Two natives, one to drive and another to counsel the driver—Mynheer Johannes, that is our fat friend—'Bros and ourselves went along the road to Dompo. The cooking utensils, clothes and camp beds had gone on earlier packed on ponies.

At Dompo, Mynheer Johannes said that the Sultan of Dompo would visit us, but when by nine o'clock he had not come we prepared to go to bed. I was in my kimono and Talbot in his pyjamas when he suddenly appeared. Our attire, however, seemed in no way to displease him, for when at his request the gun case and the rifle case were opened, he verily danced with excitement as he handled the weapons. He took them to pieces and cleverly put them together, adopted a vagrant matchbox within his reach, opened and shut again and again the folding chairs we had brought. The guns meanwhile had been put away, but they had to come out again for his pleasure. At last he left us, promising to take us hunting the next day.

Early we rode forth for deer, the usual Dutch Indies procedure of beating the surrounding country being here adopted. Three stags were grassed, Talbot getting two of them as they rushed through the thicket, driven by men and hounds.

With the evening came the Sultan's tea-party. Oh ! It was a lovely tea-party ! First we entered the long wooden house, the whole length of it one noble room, with coloured hangings and carved windows, and a round table and a few chairs at the top of this hall. The Sultan was in the place of honour, and now he was quiet and dignified. A serving boy sat cross-legged on the floor beside him with a golden box, containing the foot-long native cigarettes made of home-grown tobacco and rolled in tobacco leaf. I sat on the Sultan's right. I was dressed in white, with a cape of wonderful French tissue, more beautiful than any Eastern silks. Beyond me were Talbot and Falstaff, and beyond them the household of the Sultan. The men sat cross-legged and naked to the waist, armed with " Krisses," silently watching us. Opposite me was the young Rajah, schooled, pensive and spectacled, his mind enslaved by the West, his soul by the East, torn between to-day and yesterday, between Europe and Asia. He had been brilliant at college in Java, but had not finished his studies, for he was married now, at the age of nineteen. A Mahommedan priest sat beyond him in ample white garments telling his beads —thirty-three beads to ask for pardon, thirty-three to pray for gifts and graces, and thirty-three to praise Allah, for He is great ; ninety-nine in all. Then came in bronze-coloured men, tall and silent, half-naked. half-clothed in rainbow sarongs. They carried trays of cakes and cups of coffee. The generous table was covered with delicious things.

I told the Sultan of the magic of the West, of men flying in the air, and living under the sea, and killing each other sixty miles away. The sun set, the time came for the evening prayer—the fifth time for praying in the day—therefore we went away.

We walked home through the little village where no women were seen save a few, veiled to the eyes, bringing in pitchers of water. We passed ponies bathing and drinking in the river, and massive buffaloes. This island is the home of horses and of cattle, and they are its wealth.

The next morning we were away by six o'clock. The motor car could go no further owing to the state of the road, and we had a journey of thirty-six hours before us.

The ponies were so small that Talbot helped his along by using his walking stick as he would have used it had he been on foot. At one o'clock we arrived at the next bivouac, exhausted by the heat that was so great that after lunch we could not even sleep. Our luggage followed us, packed upon ponies, and not carried by men as in Celebes. A slight hot breeze had blown masses of dust upon us. At the appointed hour for our next progress, which was that of the rising of the full moon, and when the watchman had beaten on his long beam of wood the passing of the tenth hour, we rode out again. We passed " sawas," wide fields, full of neighing tethered stallions, and went by others, where mares and their foals were grazing in the low, irrigated places where green food can grow.

After an hour's solemn amble we found ourselves by the seashore of the Gulf of Salee. Two great bamboo outriggers awaited us, one of them for 'Bros and the luggage, and one for ourselves and for the native who now replaced Mynheer Johannes as our interpreter with the dialect-speaking people. We had to call this man the " Jerubasa ! "

A slight wind blew as we undertook our night journey, which could not be made by day as the winds are then most dangerous. The vicious squalls that sweep down from the mountains wreck any frail craft they encounter. Our men sometimes rowed and sometimes sailed. The sail was made by hand of palm fibre. I slept happily upon the wooden board, or waked to watch the sea and Venus shining until the sun replaced her loveliness.

We were carried ashore at Labuan Jumbo and had a painful walk in the heat to the Rest House of Ampang. The Jerubasa had wearied of us and left us, but we found a Swiss overseer who was directing the building of a bridge. He was asleep on a bare table.

A fire was burning and smoking right in front of the house. Before cooking the meal of venison which we shared with him, I asked the Swiss why the fire was there, the cause of heat and smoke to him. He said : " The fire is nearer there than it would be in the kitchen." This answer, and the use of a table in lieu of a bed, spoke loudly of the man's weariness of the East. What matter a little more discomfort when all was so discomfortable ?

Each day, for three days, we rode twenty miles. Twenty miles to Plampang, and twenty miles to Lapé, and twenty more to Sumbawa. The thermometer in a leather box registered 104 degrees ; my body seemed to note an even greater heat. We took from six to seven hours each day, sometimes along paths and sometimes along a road with a stone foundation. This road was pulled to pieces, stones were thrown up and deep holes were made by the wild pigs of the jungle.

Shut your eyes and see through mine the sun-baked hills, pink in the morning and the evening ; the many goats, ponies and buffaloes that eat only parched rice stalks and scrub and yet are mysteriously fat! See the group of grey monkeys, unafraid as we passed ; there is one scratching himself on a tree, another is examining the dust upon the road, whilst others squeal and fight among the branches of the low trees. Be gladdened by the golden orioles, the white cockatoos, and by the little blue birds of the jay family that live in the ground in holes about ten inches long. Imagine too the jungle fowl that strut across the road, seeming to revel in this waterless land. They a little resemble pheasants, and the male crows like a young domestic cock as he marshals sometimes one mate, sometimes two, before him. Talbot stalks and shoots them, and thereby assures us of a meal when this long road is over. Come with us through the dry river beds, full of stones, with here and there green slimy water holes. You, too, must cross the bridges made only of palm matting slung above wooden piles. You must enter the queer untidy villages palisaded against the wild pigs, the " unclean beasts " that the people, being Mahommedans, will not eat, nor even touch, unless, perhaps, they are sometimes tempted by the Dutch Government's offer of two shillings for every pig's tail. The pigs destroy the crops, and it is decreed that they shall be destroyed.

At the end of our fourth day of riding in the sun we reached Sumbawa, the western port that was our destination.

For three days we enjoyed this hamlet. To Mynheer Schol we owed our pleasure. He was the Government veterinary surgeon, who oversaw the buffaloes and the ponies exported to Java and elsewhere. He told me that he had never seen a pony of Sumbawa with bad feet. Mynheer Schol showed us his ponies, and took me driving in his two-wheeled buggy over the bad roads, through a dry river bed, dashing along at twelve miles an hour, with constant shying and prancing.

In Port Sumbawa was another Sultan, and another tea-party. Again the gun and rifle were examined and their prices asked, and when given not believed ! After that came the everlasting Eastern question to Talbot : " How old are you ? " followed by wild guesses as much as fifteen years out, because his white hair combined with his activity greatly puzzled his questioners. Followed then their pleasant satisfaction when they were told his age. I puzzled them with my : " How old am I ? " A courtier, even in Sumbawa, plays his part, and one of them at once answered, " Twenty-five," at which I laughed so gaily that every code of an Eastern Court was broken ; next I told this gallant the sorry unromantic truth.

Our host had a green velvet jacket and trousers, and

ONE OF MYNHEER SCHOL'S PONIES.

SCENE IN SUMBAYA.

Photographs by Violet Clifton.

To face page 274.

between them, in spite of jewels and a big buckle, his stomach gleamed out.

The young Rajah looked dignified in silver and black, and all the family was of a type at once delicate, proud and aristocratic. The long spacious room with its gold-coloured pillars, its empty frames on the wall, and a large bed and some European furniture, was pleasing in the half light. A long, wooden descent led from the single storied house to some benches below, where often the family sat.

The young Rajah and other gentlemen of Sumbawa took us and Mynheer Schol on splendid ponies out into the hills to hunt. Talbot stalked with a native and got two wild pig, which convicts later took back to the town. No one else would bear such defilement. After sunset he stalked again with a lamp, but it was too early in the night for the deer to go to the stream to drink.

The country " ghillie " took us to a field wherein grazed many of his own ponies. In a far spot we saw a wild pig sleeping. The ghillie held up the lamp, and in its sole light, Talbot shot and killed the beast at sixty yards range, which was a fine shot and greatly delighted the people. The ghillie had shown fear lest one of his ponies be shot, but when he saw the detested tusker slain he became most joyful. The young Rajah and his uncles were hunting elsewhere but got nothing. Late at night by the light of several fires we all rested together on mats that had been brought up for the feast. We had fruit and cakes to eat, whilst we told the Rajah about the red deer of the

Highlands.   After this we rode back in the dark, warm night, down steep rocky paths, and finally home with a splendid gallop.

Mynheer Schol told us on our return why he had avoided the Rajah's uncles, which aloofness I had noticed as we lay and ate fruit in the firelight.   One of them, it is strongly suspected, was the cause of the former Dutch veterinary surgeon and his wife being murdered whilst they were driving in the country. This royal chieftain does not like Europeans.

On the 28th September, the ship *Van Riemsdyk* took us from Sumbawa, the first place in our travels which we both regretted leaving.   Sailing across the Strait of Allas, we next day reached Laboehanhadji, a port on the island of Lombok.

CHAPTER XXX

THE ISLAND OF LOMBOK

" Blessed of the Lord be his land . . . And for the chief
things of the ancient mountains, and for the precious things
of the lasting hills.'

Deut. xxxiii. 13-15.

WE crossed the straits of Allas on the s.s. *Van Riemsdyk.*
On one side of the deck was a long line of ponies, on
the other a long line of buffaloes, but it takes more than
several hundred head of such animals to make any
sort of unpleasant smell on a Netherlands' steamer.
Therefore, our four-legged passengers were altogether
pleasant and lovely to us as we neared Lombok, which
rose sheer out of the sea in a superb sweep of upland
coast.

I thought of Wallace and of his observation that
Lombok is the frontier where Asia ends and Australasia begins. Here, we shall see, or if not, shall
at least know, that we have as neighbours cockatoos,
megapods, and quaint bee-eaters and ground thrushes,
all creatures of Australasia. After we have sailed
through the Straits of Lombok and refound Bali, we
shall be back amongst those beings to which Asia
is mother.

Although I loved Sumbawa because of our fine

gallops there, and because of the arid stretches of land, the ponies, the buffaloes, the strutting jungle fowl and the still potent Sultans, yet, after its dryness, Lombok was enchanting. Sumbawa has only two months' monsoon in the year, but in spite of its long, rainless season, in a stretch of twelve months it shipped 20,000 ponies away to other islands. Lombok is entirely different, and it caused me vivid emotion. I never saw scenery like to it. It is in truth a garden island. Lombok covers over three thousand square miles. It rises to majesty in the north in the great Peak of Lombok, nearly 12,000 feet high; then, again, in the south is a range of mountains, and in between lie jungle, lesser hills and long rich valleys, with terraces and fields. It rejoices in a Garden of Eden beauty and fertility. From times long past have come down the arts of irrigation and of husbandry. Perhaps inconsequently the Koranic saying ran in my head : " For the wife is the husband's tillage." Here the earth resembles an adored wife, fruitful to her lord. Four times a year the " sawas " give forth their crops, maize, rice, tobacco, onions, in successive wealth. Think of this, you farmers of England ! All is green, watered with springs and rivers carefully and skilfully led into many channels. " Twenty-five piculs of rice that field will yield me," said a Malay-speaking Sasak farmer as I stood looking at an acre of fecundity. In Java such a space of earth would yield about five piculs of rice, and no such succession of crops would be yielded by the same ground.

The population of the centre of the island is a

mixture of the eastern and the western peoples, for in the west there are many Balinese, and people who live under Balinese influence are Hindu by religion. The domination of the Balinese was broken by the Dutch in the Battle of Matoram, but individual Balinese still own some of the " sawas." They are too proud to work on the land, so the men of Lombok lease the fruitful acres and grow richer than the landowners. Different tongues as well as different creeds mark the various divisions in Lombok. The Lombok Balinese of the western part and the Sasaks, the original, now Mahommedan, population of the eastern part seldom inter-marry.

As we journeyed west, we passed a village where live young women who will not readily marry a youth unless he be a stealer of cattle. In three years three hundred youths—so I was told by a Netherlands official—had gone thence to Java exiled for theft. They enjoy the journey and the sight of a new country and the opportunity of learning to speak Malay.

Lombok, I said, caused me emotion. I took joy in the fertility, the verdure, the scent of the aromatic herbs, and the flowering tobacco. Then, to crown all, on the second day of our too short sojourn in Lombok we came upon Normada—Normada the unexpected, the hidden, the wonderful.

Normada is a village. We knew that there we should find a Rest House, where we meant to spend two nights. We arrived hot and dusty, and I thought that probably I should have at once to oversee the cooking. Instead of drudgery in a Rest House, we found a palace—not a mere Palace, but a most lovely palace, set in a garden, like a house in a dream.

There were tiny windows and long gallery rooms ; the doors were carved and were lacquered red. The floors were golden and blue, as are perhaps the floors of Heaven. It was enchanting. I shall never forget my odd little bedroom, nor the long verandah where I sat looking into the terraced garden with great, cool water tanks, and crotons of every colour. Nor shall I cease, in pleasant leisure, to remember the Hindu temples that crowned the summits of the garden, and the priest of Bali who burnt incense, chanted, and toyed with magnolia flowers, and talked with me when the garden was quiet in the sunset hour.

I wished only that the late Sultan, now exiled in Bali, might too be here, because he was good and wise, and this was his house. He was banished by the Dutch because he would not reign on in righteousness unless his sons should come after him. His sons were full of oppression and of cruelty and the Dutch forbade their succession. So he was sent to Bali with two of his wives. His eldest son was killed fighting the conquerors, and the second one killed himself, whilst the third one became half mad. His youngest lives in Bali and studies his religion. He once came back to the Palace in Lombok and wondered to see white people in the house of his fathers.

Then we had to leave Normada in the foolish way we leave all the loveliest places, instead of living there

"COOL WATER TANKS"

To face page 280.

happily ever afterwards, as we should do if life were really a fairy tale.

We went to Mataram, the place of fighting, and then to Ampenan, whence we sailed for Bali.

Isle of wealth, of verdure, and of terraced valleys, good-bye !

CHAPTER XXXI

THE RETURN

"The world has no such flower in any land,
And no such pearl in any gulf the sea,
As any babe on any mother's knee!"

SWINBURNE.

THE voyage towards Bali was beautiful ; the island rose
very tall and slim above the sunset-coloured sea, and
a flight of white ibis revived memories of Bali.

Early next day we landed at Boelelen and saw again
the coconut trees. A procession was carrying a
wooden god in a box, but gone from my eyes was the
glamour that had made my heart beat with joy when
I had landed in Bali earlier in the year. Bali looked—
alas ! that I write it—tawdry. I knew that it was time
that I should return west—that I should go to where
life is harder and more complicated, less materially
easy, spoiled by a hundred complexities. Yet there
the poor man, selling newspapers in the street, the girl
at the monotonous counter, have a light, a quickness, a
response in their eyes, that I had not seen in Eastern
eyes. The charm of childhood is here, of the wild,
undeveloped ; there, West, is the magic of intellect, of
activity, of character. I longed for the light on the
hills that would show amethyst and topaz in place of
this ruby and emerald of the East. I wanted soft

mists and tender blues instead of the crude elementary green, and shadows too intense. My body was tired with heat and the long way; I longed for my children and for rest.

Passing Surabaya, that busy part of Northern Java, I noted some days later in my diary: " It is strange, and a little sad, to see the Javanese caught in the wheel of our Western activities; coming from further East, Bali was the last outpost of the calm of the Orient."

Many curious things had we seen, and now was ended this chapter of our lives.

POSTSCRIPT

READING this through, I said to Talbot : " Strange, is it not, that in spite of so many warnings, so many predictions of evil, yet, in these long travels, we had no adventures that we did not surmount." He said : " Dangers vanish before one who knows. Take a revolver where none should be taken and all may be lost ; hesitate, listen overmuch to advice, and every obstacle becomes a barrier, the journey is never carried through." Something like this he said, and I realised that he has a genius for exploration. He can express his nature in far journeys. Difficulties overcome, sulky natives made friendly, all these are as so many spoils to the hunter. Often adventure is the fruit of ignorance. The mind does not calculate or foresee the difficulties of a campaign or of an expedition, and then the body suffers and has misfortunes. Courage perforce steps in where provision failed. The chronicles of ancient explorers prove this. Most of their adventures hinged on their mistakes and miscalculations.

Keyserling truly says : " There is no greater superstition than the belief in the unsurmountability of natural conditions. Nature, of course, is as she is—the facts of Nature are doubtless insuperable in themselves ; but all forces are effective only upon a certain plane, and the man who rises above it escapes their influence. He does not escape these forces in imagination but in absolute reality, because, ' knowing better ' presupposes ' becoming different.' In his deepest being, man is spirit, and the more he recognises this, the more firmly he believes it, the more fetters fall away from him."

I read this by Keyserling and the book fell from my hand—yes, that was it ! I had, when crossing Celebes, enslaved my body, which is not entirely strong. I had drawn on myself as a spirit. Talbot " knew better," so the fetters fell, and thus with safety we attained our end.

INDEX